Rain of (

The Stages of the Path in the Sakya Tradition

Lama Jampa Thaye

Dechen Foundation

Dechen Foundation is a 501(3)(c) nonprofit organization registered in the State of California.

ISBN 978-0-9987507-7-4

Contents

Foreword by H.H. 41st Sakya Trizin

His Holiness
Sakya Trizin
HEAD OF THE SAKYAPA ORDER
OF TIBETAN BUDDHISM

Dolma Phodrang
192 Rajpur Road
P.O. Rajpur 248009
Dehra Dun U.A. INDIA

For some time, Lama Jampa Thaye has endeavoured, through his teachings and writings, to take the dharma to Western devotees in a form that supports them in implementing the principles of Buddhist philosophy in their lives. It is a pleasure to introduce his latest effort in propagating the dharma.

This work is intended as a gateway into Buddhist spiritual thought as a basis for a healthy and spiritually fulfilled life. In it, Lama Jampa Thaye covers the Buddhist path from the initial taking refuge right up to the profound teachings of the vajrayana. He deals with the Buddhist object of refuge — the Three Jewels; the developing of the correct motivation — bodhichitta; the principles of behaviour in the path — the six perfections; the correct view — understanding emptiness; and concludes by introducing the vajrayana vehicle. Through this teaching, the student receives a full blueprint of entering the path, keeping the vows, maintaining motivation, leading a better and more virtuous life, and finally a way to liberation.

Lama Jampa Thaye introduces the Buddhist teachings in the light of modern scientific thought and contemporary life. This makes the work useful for the new practitioner, creating a bridge between their current understanding and the profound dharma.

Finally I would like to commend Lama Jampa Thaye for the unflagging enthusiasm and effort that he has devoted to the noble cause of making the dharma available to all those who have an interest in it, and encourage him to continue his good works.

His Holiness Sakya Trizin
Sakya Dolma Phodrang, Rajpur, India
31st May, 2005

Foreword by
Karma Thinley Rinpoche

ཀ་ཁས་དབང་དུ་མ་ཅུ་མས་པ་མཐའ་ཡས་ཀྱིས་
མཛད་པའི་འདུལ་ལྟུན་ས་སྐྱའི་ལྟ་དགོངས་གཞིར་བཞག་སྟེག་
པ་གསུམ་ཀྱི་གྲུབ་མཐའ་ཁ་གསལ་ལ་ཉམས་ལེན་གྱི་སོར་མཛད་
པ་འདིས་མདོ་སྔགས་བསྟན་ལ་སློབ་གཉེར་ཡོངས་ལ་ཕན་པ་རྒྱ་
ཆེར་ཡོང་རེས་དེ་བཞིར་སྔགས་ལ་རེས་འཆལ། སྙེ་ར་བཞི་པའི་
ཚེས་དང་པོ་དགེ་བར། ཀརྨ་ཕྲིན་ལས་བཞི་མིང་པས། ལོན་ཊོན་
སྔུན་ཚོགས་དགེ་ལེགས་ཀྱིས་བརྒྱན་པའི་གྲོང་ཁྱེར་ཆེན་པོར་བྲིས་པ་
དགེ་ལེགས་འཕེལ།

This book, written by the Lord of Scholars, Jampa Thaye, is concerned with the distinct tenets and practices of the three vehicles based on the view of Shri Sakya. Since it will bring extensive benefits to students serious about the sutra and mantra doctrines, I request it be taken to heart.

This was written on the good first day of April by the one named the Fourth Karma Thinley, in London, the great city adorned with abundant goodness. May virtues increase.

Introduction

Nowadays there is considerable interest in the Sakya school of Buddhism but, regrettably, only a limited number of books on this tradition and its spiritual teachings exist in Western languages. Thus the present work has been written to introduce the principal points of the Sakya system of exposition and practice to a modern audience.

The Sakya tradition itself takes its name from the monastery founded at Sakya in south-western Tibet in 1073 by Könchok Gyalpo of the Khön clan, an influential family that had previously been affiliated to the Nyingma tradition of Buddhism. As a result of his family's disillusionment with errors that had begun to affect contemporary Buddhist practice in Tibet, Könchok Gyalpo studied the 'new tantras' with the translator Drokmi Lotsava, one of the most influential Tibetan scholars of that period. Subsequently the Sakya school was given definite shape through the labours of the 'five venerable masters', Sachen Künga Nyingpo (1092-1158), Lopön Sönam Tsemo (1141-1182), Jetsün Drakpa Gyaltsen (1147-1216), Chöje Sakya Pandita (1182-1251) and Chögyal Phakpa (1235-1280). Their endeavours ensured that the Sakya tradition was endowed with an unparallelled range of sutra and mantra teachings from

Indian Buddhism. Since that time the tradition and its two major subsects, Ngor and Tsar, have been adorned by many other accomplished scholars and meditators such as Ngorchen Künga Zangpo (1382-1456), Tsarchen Losal Gyamtso (1502-1566) and Jamyang Khyentse Wangpo (1820-1892). Through the work of such luminaries the Sakya school has exerted an enormous influence on the development of religious, cultural and political life in Tibet and elsewhere.

The head of the Sakya tradition is drawn from the male line of the Khön family. The present head, His Holiness the Kyabgon Gongma Trizin, Ratna Vajra Rinpoche (1974-), hails from the Dolma Palace branch of the dynasty and is the forty-second Sakya Trizin ('holder of the Sakya throne'). In 2017 he succeeded his father, Kyabgon Gongma Trichen Rinpoche, Ngawang Künga Thegchen Palbar Samphel Wanggi Gyalpo (1945-) who, in exile from Tibet, established his primary seat in Rajpur in northern India.

1

Taking Refuge
in the Three Jewels

The foundation of spiritual practice is the existence within all beings of buddha nature. It is this which motivates one to seek liberation and enlightenment.

As Maitreya says:

> If there were no buddha nature, there would be no discontent with suffering, nor desire, effort and aspiration for nirvana.[1]

This innate disposition to buddhahood is none other than the primordial nature of one's mind. However, mind is presently veiled by the two obscurations, the first being that of the disturbing emotions and the second being that of nescience in regard to ultimate reality. Yet, despite these veiling factors, mind remains fundamentally pure, since, being adventitious, the obscurations do not form part of its actual nature. Thus, when the mind meets with the skilful methods of the spiritual path, one is motivated to practise, the obscurations are progressively stripped away and the state of buddhahood, supreme enlightenment, results.

One enters onto that path by means of the ceremony of 'taking refuge in the Three Jewels', namely the Buddha, dharma and the sangha. In this ritual one becomes a member of the community (sangha) which practises the teachings (dharma) given by the supremely accomplished teacher (Buddha) and, from this time onward, one relies on the Three Jewels for refuge from the threefold suffering of misery, change and conditionality.

As Lopön Sönam Tsemo says:

> It is called refuge because it protects from obscurations, fear and suffering.[2]

The significance of designating the Buddha, dharma and sangha as 'the Three Jewels' is that, like precious gems, they possess both rarity and sublimity.

In this respect Maitreya describes them as follows:

> Their occurrence is rare; they are free from defilements;
> They possess power; they are the adornment of the
>   world;
> They are sublime and they are unchanging.
> Thus they are rare and sublime.[3]

There are five principal factors involved in the act of taking refuge:

1. The motivation for taking refuge
2. The objects in which one takes refuge

3. The method of taking refuge
4 The training that follows taking refuge
5. The benefits of taking refuge

In addition, an outline of the pratimoksha vow is appended here to these five topics, since whoever has taken refuge is thereby qualified to receive this vow.

1. The motivation for taking refuge

It is commonly said that there are three motivations for taking refuge: fear, faith and compassion.

As Ngorchen Könchok Lhündrup says:

> To begin, the three causes of seeking refuge are fear, faith and compassion.[4]

A. Fear

Since the basic characteristic of existence in the cycle of birth and death is suffering due to the disturbing emotions and their ensuing karmic activity, one takes refuge in the Three Jewels, which are the only objects that provide reliable protection from such misery.

Gyalse Thokme Zangpo says:

> If even he is trapped in the prison of samsara,
> What worldly god has the power to give refuge?
> Therefore when seeking protection, to go for refuge
> To the undeceiving Three Jewels is the practice of a
>   Conqueror's child.[5]

B. Faith

Three types of faith lead one to take refuge in the Three Jewels: clear faith, longing faith and convinced faith. 'Clear faith' is the inspiration that one experiences in beholding representations of the Three Jewels or hearing of the qualities of the Buddha and his teaching. 'Longing faith' is the earnest desire to acquire these qualities and 'convinced faith' is being certain about the truth of Buddha's teachings on action, cause and effect and the four noble truths of suffering, its cause, cessation of suffering and its cause, which doctrines comprise the essential basis of the dharma.

C. Compassion

One takes refuge with compassion when, understanding that misery afflicts all beings, one wishes to assist them by relying on the aid of the Three Jewels. However, one should not confuse this altruistic motivation for taking refuge with the generation of bodhichitta, the very core of the Great Vehicle, to be discussed later.

As Lopön Sönam Tsemo comments:

> If one asks whether taking refuge and generating bodhichitta are distinct, the answer is that they are, because bodhichitta is the promise to attain enlightenment for the benefit of others.[6]

2. The objects in which one takes refuge

As has already been established, the actual objects in which one takes refuge are the Buddha, dharma and sangha.

However, since the dharma itself was set forth by Lord Buddha in two distinct presentations, the Lesser and Great Vehicles, there are two ways in which the nature of the Three Jewels themselves is explained.

In the Lesser Vehicle the jewel of Buddha is synonymous with Buddha Shakyamuni, the Sage of the Shakyas. The jewel of dharma is twofold, being both the 'dharma of the scriptural tradition', taught by Lord Buddha and consisting of the three 'baskets' of scriptures, namely the vinaya (discipline), abhidharma (higher teaching) and sutra (discourses), and the 'dharma of realisation', which itself consists of the truths of the cessation of suffering and the path to cessation. The jewel of the sangha comprises both the 'ordinary' sangha, consisting of four or more ordained disciples, and the 'noble' sangha, consisting of those who have attained the level of a 'noble being', one who, as his designation indicates, has decisively cut his connection with samsara.

In the Great Vehicle the jewel of Buddha comprises both the dharmakaya ('the truth body'), by which the benefit of self is accomplished, and the rupakaya ('the form body'), by which the benefit of others is accomplished. As in the Lesser Vehicle, the jewel of dharma comprises both 'scriptural tradition' and 'realisation'. However, here 'scriptural tradition' includes the extensive discourses in which Lord Buddha set forth the Great Vehicle. The jewel of sangha comprises both the 'noble' sangha and the 'ordinary' sangha. In this vehicle, the 'noble sangha' includes not only those who have achieved one of the stages of a noble being on the shravaka ('disciple') or pratyekabuddha ('solitary realiser') paths of the Lesser Vehicle but also those who have attained one of the ten levels on the bodhisattva path of the Great Vehicle. The 'ordinary' sangha is constituted by all those who have taken refuge before oneself. Furthermore, from amongst these Three Jewels it is the jewel of Buddha that constitutes the definitive object of refuge. This is so because a Buddha is endowed with the dharmakaya, resulting from his apprehension of the true nature of reality. The jewel of dharma is, by contrast, merely the means to achieve this apprehension and the sangha consists of those following the path of the dharma.

On this point Lord Maitreya has stated:

> The dharma will be abandoned and is of an unsteady nature. It is not the ultimate and the sangha is still fearful. Thus the two aspects of dharma and the noble assembly do not represent the supreme refuge, which is constant and stable. Ultimately only the Buddha is the refuge of beings, since the Great Sage possesses the dharmakaya and the assembly reaches its ultimate goal there.[7]

As an addendum to this discussion of the objects of refuge, it should be noted that in the vajrayana, the extraordinary part of the Great Vehicle, the lama who bestows the requisite initiations, transmissions and instructions is considered to be the embodiment of the Three Jewels.

As it says in the tantras:

> The lama is the Buddha; the lama is the dharma.
> Likewise the lama is the sangha.
> All their activities are the lama.[8]

Sakya Pandita says:

> However good he may be,
> A teacher who belongs to the shravaka tradition
> Is just an ordinary person, while one
> Of the perfections system is, if good,
> The jewel of the noble community.
> An excellent master of the mantra system
> Is none other than the Three Jewels.[9]

It is also taught in the vajrayana that the lama, yidam and dakini constitute the 'inner refuge'. In this respect the lama who bestows teachings is the 'root of blessings'; the yidam-deity upon which one meditates is the 'root of siddhis'; and the dakinis, whose inspiration accompanies one on the path, are the 'root of activities'.

3. Method

The first time that one takes refuge is on the occasion of participating in the ceremony conducted by one's lama or a senior member of the sangha. The ritual itself is drawn from the vinaya, it being Lord Buddha himself who instituted refuge as the initial mode of entry into the sangha.

In this ceremony one takes refuge in the Buddha as one's teacher, since he is 'supreme among humans', in the dharma as one's path, since it is 'supreme in its freedom from attachment' and in the sangha as one's companions on the path, since it is 'supreme among assemblies'. Furthermore, here in the 'ordinary' refuge ceremony one takes refuge 'until the end of this life', but later in the 'extraordinary' refuge, which must precede the ritual generation of bodhichitta in the ceremony of the bodhisattva vow, one will take refuge 'until the achievement of the essence of enlightenment'.

On this point Sakya Pandita says:

> Worldly refuge is taken simply for one's own benefit and happiness in this and future lives, not until the essence of enlightenment or even as long as one lives. Shravakas and pratyekabuddhas take refuge for the duration of their lives but not until the essence of enlightenment. Bodhisattvas take refuge until they obtain enlightenment.[10]

4. Training

After taking refuge one should avoid three negative actions, the commission of which would be contradictory to the nature of the Three Jewels.

The 'great charioteer' Asanga describes these actions as follows:

> Whoever has taken refuge in the Buddha must not take refuge in other gods; whoever has taken refuge in the dharma must not harm sentient beings; whoever has taken refuge in the sangha must not pay reverence to followers of other systems.[11]

Despite the straightforwardness of this injunction, it might be wondered whether refuge might be given to followers of other religions. Such an action would be mistaken, since a follower of a theistic tradition takes refuge in his particular divinity and not in Buddha, 'the teacher of both gods and men'. The same point equally applies to the notion that, for example, one could be both a Buddhist and a Christian. Only someone for whom reason and language have neither meaning nor value could say such a thing, for there is an unbridgeable gap between the Buddhist denial of a creator and the claim, common to all theistic traditions, that such a creator actually exists. Just as both these views cannot simultaneously be right, so one cannot simultaneously be a Buddhist and a Christian. Needless to say, this does not contradict the obligation to be kind towards all beings and to appreciate whatever is virtuous in others' religious or philosophical systems.

To implement the positive aspect of training, one should recite the verses of refuge at least seven times each day, make offerings to the Three Jewels and always show respect to objects which represent them, such as images, scriptural texts and the colours of the monastic robes. Such practices constitute the most basic training.

However, for those who wish to make rapid progress on the path, a more extensive training is required. This involves the threefold process of listening to the dharma, reflecting upon its meaning and meditating to accomplish it.

Sakya Pandita summarised this training as follows:

In brief, you should hear, think and meditate on the teachings spoken by the Buddha, compiled by his disciples, practised by the siddhas, expounded by the great scholars, translated by qualified translators and taught by skilful teachers. Any other teaching, though seeming to be profound, is not the true buddhadharma and is not fit to be the object of hearing, thinking and meditating.[12]

For those who are unsure what is to be accepted as the teaching of the Buddha, Lord Maitreya, regent of Shakyamuni, has given the following definition:

> Whatever speech is meaningful and well connected
>   with dharma,
> Which removes all defilements of the three realms
> And shows the benefits of peace,
> Is the speech of the Sage, while any speech differing
>   from this is that of another.[13]

Similarly, one should heed Maitreya's words on what is to be accepted as an authoritative commentary:

> Whatever someone has explained with an undistracted
>   mind
> Exclusively in the light of the Conqueror's teaching
> And conducive to the path of attaining liberation,
> One should revere as the words of the Sage.[14]

While the sutras and tantras expounded by Lord Buddha are the authentic sources of the teachings, one must rely exclusively upon inferential reasoning and direct experience as the means of acquiring certainty in the truth of those teachings. In this respect the buddhadharma stands apart from those religious systems which claim that their scriptural traditions are self-validating and thus immune to reasoning.

Concerning the nature and role of reasoning, Mipham Rinpoche says:

> By the science of logic one comes to know the manner in which certain predicates are established or not established from a certain proof.[15]

However, those who claim the mantle of Buddhism but propound views directly contrary to the teachings of the Buddha are, ipso facto, unworthy of respect as expounders of the dharma. They would benefit from hearing the following injunction of Lord Maitreya:

> There is no one in this world more skilled in the dharma than the Conqueror.
> No other has such insight, knowing everything without exception and knowing supreme thusness the way it is.
> Thus one should not distort the discourses presented by the Sage himself,
> Since this would destroy the Sage's mode of teaching and, furthermore, cause harm to the sacred dharma.[16]

If, for instance, someone were to deny the truth of rebirth, it would be in contradiction to Buddha's own words on this topic. Furthermore, such a mistaken notion would be at odds with the whole of Lord Buddha's teaching, whether it be the preciousness of human birth, the validity of karma and morality or the purpose of the bodhisattva career and the possibility of buddhahood itself.

In passing, it should be mentioned here that the reasoning which establishes the reality of rebirth is well-known to scholars within the dharma. Great masters such as Dharmakirti have exposed the impossibility inherent in materialist theories of the origin of consciousness which assert, in contradiction to reason, that a material and non-sentient cause can generate a non-material and sentient effect. Through this immaculate reasoning one is left with only rebirth as an adequate explanation of the phenomenon of consciousness.

As Mipham Rinpoche says:

> Since the present consciousness is seen to occur and continue from the previous consciousness, its own perpetuating cause, it is impossible that it should arise from matter without its own former perpetuating cause. This would be like a sprout arising from stone or light from darkness.[17]

Concerning the actual transmission of the dharma, as Sakya Pandita has maintained above, one receives the scriptural teachings of the jewel of dharma directly from 'skilful teachers'. For this reason, even when one cannot obtain a detailed explanation of a particular scriptural text from one's master, one should at least try to obtain the 'reading transmission' (Tib. lung, Skt. agama) from him, for this conveys the blessing inherent in the teaching. On this subject it should be said that, while the same secrecy is not required of non-tantric texts as tantric ones, nevertheless the blessing inherent in non-tantric texts is conveyed by reading transmissions.

The importance of receiving reading transmissions is demonstrated by the great lengths to which masters have always gone in order to receive them, as one can see from such histories as Gö Lotsava's *Blue Annals*, and the meticulous records kept by them, listing the reading transmissions and initiations that they have received.

On this matter Sakya Pandita's comments are apposite:

An artificial nose, a purchased son, borrowed jewellery,
Stolen goods and teacherless learning,
Although one might possess these five things,
They are not esteemed by others.[18]

5. Benefits

The benefits of taking refuge are twofold: temporary and ultimate.

The principal temporary benefit is that from the time of taking refuge one is protected from harm, both in this life and in the course of future existences. The deities who guard the four directions of the world, namely Dhritarashtra, Virudhaka, Virupaksha and Vaishravana, promised Lord Buddha that they would bestow protection on all those who took refuge in the Three Jewels. Furthermore, Lord Buddha himself declared that none of his followers would lack the necessities for life.

The ultimate benefit, according to the Lesser Vehicle, is that having taken refuge one will finally achieve the level of an arhat who has gained liberation from samsara by following the path of a shravaka or a pratyekabuddha. According to the Great Vehicle, the ultimate benefit is that one will achieve the level of a buddha, a source of benefit and bliss for all beings.

Lord Buddha himself declared in *The Saddharmapundarika Sutra* that the aforementioned achievements of those in the Lesser Vehicle are not final but are, in a sense, merely resting-places on the way to the ultimate goal, which is buddhahood:

> Those shravakas have not achieved nirvana. By thoroughly practising the bodhisattva path They will achieve buddhahood.[19]

Appendix: The pratimoksha vow

Taking refuge in the Three Jewels qualifies one to adopt the discipline of three successive vows, the maintenance of which in one's conduct and views constitutes the foundation of the path. These three vows are those of pratimoksha ('individual liberation'), the bodhisattva and the vidyadhara. The last two will be dealt with later, but it is appropriate to discuss the first vow here, since it follows refuge.

However, before going any further, it would be useful to define the general nature of a vow in dharma. Mipham Rinpoche offers a concise definition as follows:

> A 'vow' means a pledge to engage in virtue for as long as one lives.[20]

It is thus the promise to act in this way that both distinguishes and gives a special and superior force to the virtue performed as a result of a vow, in contrast to that performed without such a vow.

There are eight types of pratimoksha vow: those of a lay man, lay woman, female probationer, novice monk, novice nun, monk and nun and the vow of temporary abstinence. This last vow and the first two vows can be held by householders but the other five pertain only to renunciates, who have gone forth from the household life. In general terms it is appropriate to characterise the pratimoksha vow as belonging particularly to the Lesser Vehicle. However, although a specifically Great Vehicle form of the pratimoksha no longer survives, when a person, endowed with the bodhichitta that is the essence of that particular vehicle, maintains one of the eight disciplines of the pratimoksha, that vow becomes, in effect, the pratimoksha of the Great Vehicle.

As Sakya Pandita says:

Therefore the present day rituals
Which are endowed with bodhichitta
Are to be carried out as in the shravaka system.
In this way the eight types of pratimoksha
Will become the bodhisattva pratimoksha.[21]

The different types of pratimoksha vow taught by Lord Buddha in the fifth century B.C.E. were collected in the vinaya and then transmitted in four different lineages by the early shravaka schools known as the Sarvastivada, Sthaviravada, Mahasamghika and Sammitiya.

Subsequently eighteen schools flourished, each with its own recension of the vinaya.

As Sakya Pandita explained:

> The four fundamental communities of the shravakas
> Had four distinct vinayas
> And their canonical languages were also four:
> Sanskrit, Prakrit, Apabhramsha and Paisachi.
> The eighteen schools that developed from these
> Had eighteen vinayas.[22]

The vinaya that was subsequently brought to Tibet was that of the Sarvastivada school. The first transmission was known as the 'upper' lineage and was initiated by the great abbot Shantarakshita, who taught in Tibet in the eighth century at the invitation of the religious king Trisong Detsen. Its second transmission was termed the 'lower' lineage and this line was spread in the west of Tibet in the eleventh century by Lha Lama Yeshe Ö and the early masters of the Kadam school. The third and final transmission line was known as the 'Kashmiri' lineage because it was introduced by the Kashmiri scholar Shakyashribhadra (1140-1225). It was in this lineage of the vinaya that Sakya Pandita (1182-1251), first of the monastic masters of Sakya, was ordained by Shakyashribhadra himself.

The pratimoksha vow of a lay man or lay woman consists of five rules of training. Sakya Pandita describes them as follows:

The householder is instructed to take refuge in the Three Jewels, thus becoming a lay follower, maintaining the threefold refuge and observing the temporary abstinence vow. Then, by graded steps, he takes the first vow of not killing, the second vow of not stealing, the third vow of not lying and finally the fourth and fifth vows to abandon sexual misconduct and intoxication.[23]

In regard to the pratimoksha vow of renunciates, while the number of rules to be followed differs between the five types of renunciate, the core of their vow is the commitment to avoid the 'four defeats', the commission of any of which brings about expulsion from the sangha of renunciates. The defeats are set forth in *The Pratimoksha Sutra* as follows:

1. To take human life;
2. To take that which has not been given;
3. To have sexual intercourse;
4. To claim spiritual powers falsely.

While the five precepts of the householder and the four defeats of the renunciate are easy enough to comprehend, it might be useful nowadays to make clear that since participation in abortion brings about the destruction of human life, it falls under the remit of the first defeat of a renunciate and the first rule of training of the lay person.

In *The Pratimoksha Sutra* Lord Buddha says:

Whatever monk intentionally with his own hand destroys the life of a human or a human foetus or searches for a weapon or searches for a slayer ... and should he die by that, that monk ... is to be expelled.[24]

Jetsün Drakpa Gyaltsen reiterated this point by explaining that, for the act of killing to constitute a defeat for a lay person or renunciate, the being whose life is taken

> ...must be a human being at whatever stage of development.[25]

The reasoning behind these authoritative statements is that human life begins when consciousness mixes with the sperm and ovum at the moment of conception.

As Jamyang Khyentse Wangchuk says:

> In the womb there will be the white element from the father, the red element from the mother and, along with one's bardo consciousness, these will completely blend into one.[26]

With regard to the beginning of a new life in the instance of cloning, it should be pointed out that the manner in which consciousness becomes embodied must be the same as in the normal process of conception. All that is different is that the genetic coding in the female cell has been deleted and the normal role of the sperm is taken by a cell from the body whose genetic code it is wished to replicate. In any event, the same fusion of consciousness and the physical elements takes place, followed by the cellular division through which the new human being grows to maturity.

Thus the prohibition of taking life applies from the moment of conception onwards, be it through abortion, which as we have seen was condemned by Lord Buddha, or embryo experimentation. Although the latter is only of recent invention, it must be rejected on the same grounds as abortion. Such experimentation, including the research on stem cells extracted from human embryos, although allegedly for the benefit of humankind, is itself the use and destruction of one human being, no matter how tiny or young, for the benefit of another. One can understand from this particular example that it is essential to pay careful attention to the specific teachings of the Buddha, rather than assuming that, for instance, the modern employment of the term 'compassion' has the same sense as does its usage in dharma. Someone might, for instance, mistake self-indulgent sentimentality for the selfless compassion taught by Lord Buddha and declare that abortion is permissible if a baby is disabled. Leaving aside the question of who is to decide what is disability, it is the fundamental teaching of the Buddha that, as beings cherish their life, to deprive them of it is a non-virtuous action. Indeed, as Lord Buddha forbade his followers to encourage someone suffering to end his or her own life, how much more obvious is it that the killing of the disabled young is non-virtuous!

No matter who might excuse taking life on these spurious grounds, it would not be in accord with Buddha's teaching.

As Sakya Pandita says:

A master, too, should be perceived as a master
If he is in accord with the sutras and tantras.

However, master or not, be indifferent towards him
If he does not teach in accord with the Buddha's
    teaching.[27]

2

Generating Bodhichitta

Just as one becomes a Buddhist by the act of taking refuge, so one becomes a follower of the Great Vehicle by generating bodhichitta, the resolution to become a buddha for the benefit of all sentient beings.

As Jamyang Khyentse Wangchuk says:

> The refuge differentiates this path from the wrong paths of non-Buddhist systems. The generation of bodhichitta differentiates it from the inferior paths of the shravakas and pratyekabuddhas.[28]

The essence of bodhichitta itself is emptiness endowed with compassion. As such, it is the seed that, once sown in one's mind, germinates as the successive levels of the path of the bodhisattva, the hero whose mind is set on enlightenment, and finally flowers in buddhahood, when the wisdom of emptiness and the activity of compassion have reached their full extent.

Thus Chandrakirti describes its function in the following manner:

The shravakas and pratyekabuddhas are born from the
Great Sage.
Buddhas are born from the bodhisattvas, and
Compassion, non-dual understanding and
Bodhichitta are the causes of these children of the
Conquerors.[29]

Here bodhichitta will be discussed in the following fivefold division:

1. Conventional and ultimate bodhichittas
2. The lineages of the vow
3. The ritual of the vow
4. The training in bodhichitta
5. The benefits of bodhichitta

1. Conventional and ultimate bodhichittas

Conventional bodhichitta is the altruistic commitment to become a buddha in order to liberate all beings from cyclic existence and its three types of suffering. It is generated in the ceremony of the 'bodhisattva vow' made in the presence of one's master. Ultimate bodhichitta is the non-dual transcendental wisdom in which one directly perceives emptiness. This second type of bodhichitta does not properly arise until the path of insight, the third of the five paths that trace progress to enlightenment and, as it is the experience of the unelaborated nature of reality, unlike the conventional bodhichitta, it cannot be produced through a ritual.

As Sakya Pandita says:

> In brief, conventional bodhichitta is reliant upon others
> but ultimate bodhichitta is one's own realisation.[30]

One might wonder whether it is absolutely essential to participate in the bodhisattva vow ritual for conventional bodhichitta to arise. Actually it is not necessary in every instance because bodhichitta might naturally develop through having love and compassion towards all beings, through possessing faith in the Three Jewels and in the possibility of enlightenment and through maintaining an attitude of not harming others. Nevertheless, the ritual of the vow is usually the basis of the generation of bodhichitta since it ensures that one will henceforth guard that bodhichitta with the modesty and self-respect incumbent upon one who has entered onto the magnificent path of a bodhisattva.

As Lopön Sönam Tsemo says:

> Is it possible for the bodhichitta to arise without the
> correct ritual or is it impossible for it to do so? If one
> says that it arises without the ritual, it renders the ritual
> meaningless. On the other hand, it is an exaggeration
> to declare that it can only arise through the ritual, for,
> even in the absence of the ritual, it is possible for it to
> arise from other conditions.[31]

2. The lineages of the vow

Here we are specifically concerned with the bodhichitta of the Great Vehicle. However, it should be acknowledged that a system of generating vows focussed upon the attainment of enlightenment has existed within the Lesser Vehicle.

As Sakya Pandita says:

> Two traditions of generating the intent exist:
> That of the shravakas and that of the Great Vehicle.
> Shravakas acknowledge the three resolves
> Of arhat, pratyekabuddha and buddha.
> However, due to the decline of the shravaka tradition,
> These rituals are seldom practised.[32]

In the Great Vehicle there are two traditions of the ritual for the generation of bodhichitta or, as it is generally known, the 'ceremony of the bodhisattva vow'. These two are the lineages transmitted within the Chittamatra and Madhyamaka schools of tenets. The first was taught by the bodhisattva Maitreya and spread in India through the work of Asanga, peerless exponent of the Chittamatra. This lineage of the vow was subsequently spread in Tibet by Atisha and was maintained in the Kadam tradition founded by his student Dromtön Gyalwai Jungnay. The second lineage was taught by the bodhisattva Manjushri and spread in India by the 'great charioteer' Nagarjuna and other masters of the Madhyamaka school of tenets such as Shantideva. The latter's work *Entering the Bodhisattva Career* is actually the source of the ritual as it is currently practised.

This lineage of the vow has been maintained by the Sakya tradition. The principal difference between these two lineages resides in the qualifications of those who are to receive the vow. According to the Chittamatra system, candidates must possess one of the seven types of the pratimoksha vow (i.e. excluding the vow of temporary abstinence).

Atisha made a clear statement of this as follows:

> One who possesses one of the seven types of pratimoksha shares in the good fortune of the bodhisattva's vow but others do not.[33]

However, in the Madhyamaka system this is not a prerequisite. As Sakya Pandita says :

> Just as a seed of rice will not sprout in a cold place,
> So the Chittamatra intent will not arise in a sinful
> person
> And, just as barley will grow
> In both hot and cold places,
> So the Madhyamaka intent
> Will arise in all beings, whether or not they are sinful.[34]

As a rider to this point one should note that if, subsequent to embarking upon the bodhisattva path, one enters into the extraordinary vajrayana by receiving a major initiation of a yoga tantra or anuttarayoga tantra deity, one will also then possess the pratimoksha vow alongside the bodhisattva and vidyadhara vows. In the case of a householder this would be the pratimoksha of a lay follower.

3. The ritual of the vow

Here the main elements of the vow taught in the Madhyamaka lineage will be outlined. The initial prerequisite is to find a master suitably qualified to give the vow.

Sönam Tsemo delineates these qualifications in the following manner:

> The object to be relied upon is the spiritual friend who is learned in the Great Vehicle, engaged in the bodhisattva discipline and who will not abandon it even at the cost of his life. Furthermore, he himself has received the vow, is learned in the means of repairing it and disciplined in his own vow.[35]

The duration of this vow is until the achievement of buddhahood. In this respect the bodhisattva vow differs from any of the seven types of pratimoksha vow, the duration of which is only until the end of this life. By contrast, the bodhisattva vow is not given up at death and will continue to operate in future lives.

The actual ritual itself begins with the preliminaries, consisting of the extraordinary refuge, in which one takes refuge in the Three Jewels until the achievement of the essence of enlightenment.

The main part of the ceremony is the recitation of the verses expressing the two phases of the generation of bodhichitta. Thus one generates the 'aspiration' to become a buddha for the benefit of all beings, followed immediately by the 'application' to accomplish the stages of practice that will lead to that goal.

As Shantideva distinguishes these two aspects of bodhichitta:

In brief, bodhichitta
Should be understood to be of two types:
The mind that aspires to awaken
And the mind that applies itself to do so.
As is understood by the distinction
Between aspiring to go and actually going,
So the wise understand in turn
The distinction between these two.[36]

The actual verses of the vow as elaborated by Shantideva are as follows:

Just as the previous Sugatas
Gave birth to bodhichitta
And just as they successively dwelt in the bodhisattva
    practices,
So for the benefit of all beings I give birth to bodhichitta
And likewise I shall also
Successively follow the practices.[37]

The concluding part of the ritual is to rejoice in the benefits that bodhichitta brings to oneself and to others. As with the main verses of the ritual, the verses that express this rejoicing are drawn from Shantideva.

4. The training in bodhichitta

The training that follows the generation of bodhichitta is twofold, being concerned with both the maintenance and the strengthening of aspiration and application.

A. Aspiration

In conceiving of the ambition to achieve buddhahood, one has discovered a sense of responsibility towards all beings. In particular, in the vow itself one has made the promise to liberate them from suffering. Consequently, to let this aspiration wither through a lack of seriousness on one's part would be shameful.

As Shantideva declares:

> If, having made such a promise,
> I do not put it into action,
> Then, by deceiving every living being,
> What kind of rebirth will I take?[38]

The first cause of relinquishing one's aspiration is the discouragement that results from doubting one's ability to achieve buddhahood. To counter this, one should recollect that the potential for buddhahood exists in all beings and that, what is more, even the simplest of virtuous actions can set off a chain of events that leads to supreme enlightenment. This possibility is demonstrated in the story of the boy who could only offer some earth in the begging-bowl of the Buddha but eventually became a great emperor.

Secondly, one might lose confidence through anxiety that the results of one's virtuous acts might not come to fruition in this life. Such a fear is based upon an unrealistically short-term attitude. It fails to take account of the actual way that the effect of a particular action may well ripen after a number of lifetimes. In fact, the seeds of actions mature only when the appropriate conditions are gathered.

The final cause of the destruction of one's aspiration is to indulge in despair at the sorrows of the cycle of birth and death. However, one has promised to liberate beings from this very misery and, moreover, these beings are like one's only child. Finally, in any event, the aggregates of body and mind, the location of all sufferings, are themselves empty of intrinsic nature. This fact renders the misery itself illusory.

B. Application

One's application may be destroyed by four 'dark actions' that undermine one's capacity for positive and altruistic work. These are delineated in *The Sutra Requested by Kashyapa* as follows:

> Four actions obstruct bodhichitta. What are these four? They are deceiving one's lamas and holy people, making others ashamed for no reason, disrespecting those who have entered the Great Vehicle and falsely pretending to have bodhichitta while treating others badly.[39]

The remedy for such self-serving and deleterious behaviour is to train in the four 'white actions'. These are also described in the same source:

Four actions will ensure the continuity of bodhichitta in all future lives. What are those four? They are not telling lies, establishing all sentient beings in virtue, regarding all bodhisattvas as your teachers and praising them in the ten directions and inducing those who are mature to strive for enlightenment by convincing them of the defects of the Lesser Vehicle.[40]

5. The benefits of bodhichitta

Once bodhichitta has arisen, one is travelling to buddhahood. In that state, one will be endowed with the infinite capacity to benefit both self and others, a capacity that derives from one's acquisition of the two bodies of a buddha.

On this point Shantideva says:

All the buddhas who have contemplated for many
  aeons
Have seen it to be beneficial,
For by it the limitless masses of sentient beings
Will rapidly attain the supreme state of bliss.[41]

Since nothing else possesses the same transformative power, bodhichitta is pre-eminent among all virtues. Its power to change even the most lowly is described by Shantideva as follows:

The moment bodhichitta arises
In those fettered and weak in the jail of cyclic existence,
They will be called 'child of the Sugatas'

And will be honoured by both humans and gods of this
world.[42]

Its superiority over all other virtues is discussed in *The Sutra
Requested by Shridatta*, where it is said:

If someone were to fill all buddha-fields with jewels
and offer them to buddhas but someone else were to
generate bodhichitta, it would be the latter who would
have made the more eminent offering.[43]

3

Practising the Six Perfections

1. A general introduction

Having generated bodhichitta, one proceeds to the practice of the six perfections: giving, moral discipline, patience, effort, meditation and wisdom. By so doing one will gather the two accumulations of merit and transcendental wisdom, which lead to the achievement of buddhahood. Indeed, to adopt such an approach is to emulate Lord Buddha himself.

As it says in *The Praise of the Twelve Deeds of the Sage*:

I praise you, who having firstly developed bodhichitta,
Perfected the two accumulations of merit and
   transcendental wisdom
Through vast deeds in that time
And became the protector of beings.[44]

That the two accumulations are necessary is confirmed by Atisha, who declares:

> Therefore, through effort in the vow made by
> Bodhisattvas for pure, full enlightenment,
> The accumulations for complete enlightenment
> Will be thoroughly accomplished.[45]

To comprehend the significance of the term 'perfection' here in the Great Vehicle, the six perfections must be distinguished from ordinary virtuous behaviour. The latter is enacted with an understanding that the subject who performs the action, the object to whom it is directed and the action itself actually exist independently of one another. However, in the case of a 'perfection' the practitioner acts without conceptualising the true existence of subject, object or activity, since he recognises their mutual interdependence and lack of intrinsic nature.

As Chandrakirti comments:

> Generosity empty of gift, giver and recipient
> Is called a transcendental perfection.
> When attachment to the three arises,
> It is explained as a worldly perfection.[46]

Furthermore, ordinary virtue is prompted by the thought that the performance of such virtue will result in a measure of benefit for oneself, whereas in the case of a perfection one is motivated by the aim of ensuring the welfare of others. Therefore, the bodhisattva's virtue 'goes beyond' (Tib. pha-rol-tu-phyin-pa, Skt. paramita) the limitation of ordinary virtue. Due to its association with a mistaken view and its issuing from an inferior motivation, the latter cannot serve as a cause for the acquisition of transcendental wisdom and merit. The perfections, by contrast, derive from a combination of profound view and altruistic motivation and thus can serve as the causes of the gathering of these two accumulations, necessary for buddhahood.

A brief definition of each of the perfections is provided by Nagarjuna:

Giving is the complete giving away of one's wealth;
Morality is benefiting others;
Patience is the abandonment of anger;
Effort is to uphold virtue;
Meditation is one-pointedness, devoid of the disturbing
   emotions;
Wisdom is to ascertain the meaning of the truth.[47]

The first three perfections lead to the accumulation of merit; meditation and wisdom lead to the accumulation of transcendental wisdom; and effort is required for both accumulations. However, when making a distinction between them in terms of skilful means and wisdom, the first five perfections are regarded as facets of skilful means and the sixth alone, unsurprisingly, as belonging to the category of wisdom.

As Atisha says:

Apart from the perfection of wisdom,
All virtuous practices such as
The perfection of giving are described

As skilful means by the Conquerors.[48]

Indeed, in the absence of wisdom, the skilful perfections may be termed 'sightless', since it is only wisdom that produces the capacity to discern the path to liberation.

On this Chandrakirti says:

> Just as a whole group of blind people can easily be led
>   to the desired destination
> By a single person with eyes,
> So here also the one with wisdom takes along those
>   without the eye of wisdom
> And brings them to the state of a Conqueror.[49]

Finally, one should note that each of the six perfections is characterised by the following four particular powers:

1. Each is the remedy to a particular defect. Thus, for example, giving is the remedy to avarice.
2. Each is endowed with non-conceptual transcendental wisdom.
3. Each fulfils the wishes of sentient beings.
4. Each ripens sentient beings to follow the vehicle appropriate to them, be it that of the shravakas, pratyekabuddhas or bodhisattvas.

2. The six perfections individually

A. The perfection of giving

I. Its remedial function

Giving is the antidote to avarice, which unchecked, ripens in dissatisfaction, poverty and, finally, rebirth into the realm of ghosts.

II. Its practice

The perfection of giving comprises:

- a. Giving material objects
- b. Giving fearlessness
- c. Giving dharma

a. Giving material objects

i. As practised by a renunciate

A person who maintains the pratimoksha vow of a renunciate accomplishes the perfection of giving, not by gathering wealth to act as a sponsor in the hope of acquiring influence and fame, but by giving simple things that are appropriate to his or her monastic life.

ii. As practised by a householder

Such a person trains in a gradual manner to share his wealth in order to lessen his attachment to objects.

In respect of this Shantideva says:

At first the Guide of the World
Encourages the giving of such things as food.
Later, when accustomed to this,
One may gradually train in giving even one's own
body.[50]

However, it is imperative to distinguish pure from impure modes of giving. Only gifts made with a compassionate motivation and which are appropriate to the needs of the recipient are pure. Thus, for instance, to give poison to someone who might harm themselves or to provide arms to someone who might harm others would be examples of impure giving, while to donate food to the hungry or to supply medicines to the sick would be instances of pure giving.

This notwithstanding, in the final analysis the perfection of giving is not achieved through satiating the need of all beings for material objects. Rather it consists of the intention to give all things away.

On this point Shantideva comments:

If the perfection of generosity
Were the alleviation of the world's poverty,
Then, since some beings are starving now,
In what manner did the buddhas of the past perfect it?
The perfection of generosity is said to be
The thought to give away everything,
Together with the fruit of such an attitude.
Hence it is simply a state of mind.[51]

iii. As practised by someone who has realised the unoriginated nature of phenomena

Such a person can give even his own body when appropriate to achieve the welfare of others since, thanks to his realisation of emptiness, he is utterly devoid of any trace of self-hatred. However, if an ordinary practitioner were to make such a gift, his motivation would most likely be flawed due to the force of his defilements and consequently he would have committed the non-virtuous act of suicide.

As Shantideva says:

Before compassion is fully perfect,
Do not give your body itself.
How could that be conducive
To the welfare of self and others?[52]

b. Giving fearlessness

This form of generosity is accomplished by bestowing protection upon those in peril. It is especially important in this respect to save beings, both human and animal, from death.

c. Giving dharma

The suitably qualified practitioner can enact this type of giving by teaching the dharma. However, if someone lacking the requisite qualities were to attempt to instruct others, the results could be as catastrophic for his followers as jumping off a cliff with a madman. Thus, until one is ready to teach, it is more appropriate to practise the giving of dharma by the recitation of prayers and passages from the sutras of Lord Buddha.

III. The benefits of giving

Whoever practises pure giving creates the conditions for future wealth.

As Chandrakirti says:

Knowing that wealth arises from giving, Lord Buddha
first discoursed upon that.[53]

The final result of giving is the achievement of
buddhahood.

As Asanga says:

Thus all bodhisattvas who perfect the practice of giving
will achieve the unsurpassable, perfect, complete
enlightenment.[54]

B. The perfection of moral discipline

I. Its remedial function

The perfection of moral discipline is to avoid actions that
harm others or oneself and to strive for virtue. It is thus the
remedy to wrong behaviour and any attempt to practise the
previous perfection but to neglect moral discipline would
be likely to have an unfortunate outcome.

As Chandrakirti explains:

Generosity can ripen as wealth in the lower realms
When a person loses his legs of discipline.[55]

By contrast, moral discipline is the basis of all positive
qualities.

As Nagarjuna says:

Moral discipline is said to be the foundation of all
virtues,

Just as the earth is the support of both animate and
inanimate things [56]

II. Its practice

There are three aspects of moral discipline:

 a. The moral discipline of vows
 b. The moral discipline of virtuous deeds
 c. The moral discipline of working for others

a. The moral discipline of vows

The Lesser Vehicle, the Great Vehicle and the Vajra Vehicle
each have their own associated vows. Thus the pratimoksha
vow belongs to the Lesser Vehicle, the bodhisattva vow to
the Great Vehicle and the vidyadhara vow to the Vajra
Vehicle. However, since the six perfections are a precept of
the Great Vehicle, it is appropriate to outline the specific
discipline of the bodhisattva vow here.

According to the Chittamatra lineage there are four
downfalls, or 'actions which resemble a defeat', so-called
because they destroy one's bodhisattva vow. In addition,
there are forty-six branch downfalls which cause it to
decline. The four downfalls, which one must abjure in order
to maintain the discipline of the vow, are:

 1. To criticise another and praise oneself
 2. To refuse to share riches or the dharma
 3. To refuse to accept an apology
 4. To teach the dharma despite having abandoned
   the Great Vehicle

According to the Madhyamaka lineage there are fourteen downfalls to be avoided. However, according to this lineage, it is only the abandonment of bodhichitta itself that destroys one's bodhisattva vow. Nevertheless, as the commission of any of these 'downfalls' will cause one's vow to decline, it will be useful to list them here:

1. Stealing the wealth of the Three Jewels
2. Abandoning the precious dharma
3. Punishing a monk who has renounced his vows
4. Committing any of the five heinous actions
5. Holding wrong views
6. Destroying cities and towns
7. Teaching emptiness to those who are not ready
8. Causing those who have entered the path to buddhahood to abandon striving for perfect enlightenment
9. Causing someone who has entered the Great Vehicle to abandon pratimoksha
10. Maintaining the opinion that the path of training does not bring about the relinquishment of the disturbing emotions
11. Praising oneself and abusing others
12. Falsely claiming the realisation of the profound teaching
13. Taking an offering intended for the Three Jewels and causing a practitioner to be punished
14. Taking support intended for a meditator and giving it to someone merely intent on reciting

b. The moral discipline of virtuous deeds

One should seize every opportunity to perform virtuous deeds through body, speech and mind and, conversely, strive to eliminate non-virtuous behaviour. By so doing one will establish a supportive framework for spiritual development as these virtuous actions ripen in the creation of wholesome circumstances.

c. The moral discipline of working for others

In every situation one should endeavour to accomplish that which is genuinely beneficial for others, rather than privileging oneself.

III. The benefits of moral discipline

The temporal benefits of moral discipline are that one becomes influential and successful in one's work, and achieves happy rebirths. The ultimate benefit is that one will achieve buddhahood.

C. The perfection of patience

I. Its remedial function

The perfection of patience is an attitude of acceptance and tolerance, which acts as a remedy to the destructive force of anger, the most disabling factor in the moral life.

On this point Shantideva comments:

Whatever virtuous deeds,
Such as venerating buddhas and generosity,

Have been amassed over a thousand aeons
Will all be destroyed in one moment of anger.[57]

Not only does anger pit one against the world, it even alienates those who should be closest.

As Sakya Pandita says:

A lord must be particularly gentle.
It is not appropriate for him to become angry over a
    small matter.
Even if there is a jewel upon the forehead of a snake,
What intelligent person would stay beside it?[58]

Finally, the fully ripened fruit of anger is rebirth in hell.

However, since anger is so catastrophic in its effects, its remedy, patience, is conversely an immense force for goodness.

As Shantideva says:

There is no evil like hatred
And no discipline like patience.
Thus I should strive in various ways
To meditate on patience.[59]

Developing the ability to withstand provocations causes a far more extensive surrender of one's habitual clinging than any type of extravagant austerity. Furthermore, it renders our world a gentle and liveable place.

On this point Shantideva comments:

Where would I possibly find enough leather

With which to cover the surface of the earth?
However, wearing leather on the soles of my feet
Is the same as covering the earth with it.
Likewise it is not possible for me
To restrain the external course of things,
But if I restrain this mind of mine,
What would be the need to restrain all else?[60]

II. Its practice

There are three ways in which one can develop patience:

    a.   Patience in regard to the burden of dharma
    b.   Patience in regard to the two truths
    c.   Patience in regard to enemies

a. Patience in regard to the burden of dharma

Whatever difficulties are occasioned by one's practice of the dharma should be viewed as an opportunity to practise like the great masters of the past. Thus one could recall, for instance, that the Buddha patiently bore many years of austerity in his search for the true path and that the great scholars and translators gladly withstood the terrible rigours of travelling to India to bring the precious dharma to Tibet. In comparison, one's own present difficulties are trifling, but they will assist in one's journey to awakening.

b. In regard to the two truths

i. In regard to conventional truth

To be angry with or disappointed by the untamed behaviour of sentient beings is as unreasonable as being offended by fire's capacity to burn. Beings are driven by emotional and intellectual obscurations and hence their tendency is to abuse others. A wise person recognises this and, while learning not to put his trust in unreliable people, does not wound himself by reacting with anger to others' inevitably samsaric conduct.

ii. In regard to ultimate truth

When one examines a difficult situation with analytical insight, one cannot find a truly existent aggressor, nor victim, nor act of aggression. Since each of these appears solely in mutual dependence, one cannot posit anyone to whom one might react with anger for their apparent insult.

As Shantideva asks:

> What is there to gain and what is there to lose
> With things that are empty in this way?
> Who is there to pay me respect
> And who is there to abuse me?[61]

iii. In regard to enemies

As has already been indicated, patience is an exceptionally important virtue but without the appropriate conditions there is no likelihood of it developing. In fact, one requires the challenges provided by others' difficult behaviour to exert oneself in patience. From this one can only conclude that those who seem to be one's enemies are, in a sense, one's teachers and benefactors, precisely because their harmful behaviour stimulates us to patience. How, therefore, would it be right for one to react with aggression to what is, in its eventual outcome, a helpful action?

As Gyalse Thokme Zangpo declares:

If somebody like oneself or of lower status
Acts disrespectfully out of arrogance,
Placing them at the crown of one's head
With the devotion one has for one's lama is the practice
   of a Conqueror's child.[62]

III. Its benefits

The benefits of patience are that one lives happily, unflustered by agitation and worry. In future lifetimes one will be adorned with beauty and, finally, one will obtain the state of buddhahood.

D. The perfection of effort

I. Its remedial function

The perfection of effort is the antidote to laziness, a fault which renders all of one's aspirations redundant.

As Shantideva explains, there are three types of laziness:

… laziness, attraction to what is bad
And despising oneself out of despondency.[63]

A life lived in thrall to these types of laziness is one that is wasted. The very brevity of one's time here should cause one to exert oneself in the indefatigable pursuit of that which is virtuous.

As Nagarjuna says:

As you would extinguish a fire if it suddenly caught
hold of your clothes or head,
Just so you should strive to put an end to rebirth.[64]

II. Its practice

There are three aspects of the perfection of effort:

a. The armour of effort
b. Insatiable effort
c. Effort in application

a. The armour of effort

Whatever weariness one might feel at the labour involved in working for sentient beings, one must be resolute and unflinching, recalling the great effort exerted before one by the buddhas and bodhisattvas. To adopt such an attitude is to don the armour of effort. In particular, one must not think that such supreme beings could only accomplish their sublime deeds due to their exalted status. In reality, they were once ordinary beings like ourselves but by exerting effort they accomplished immeasurable goodness.

As Nagarjuna says:

Those who realised the truth
Neither fell from the sky nor sprang up like grain from
the earth.
They were formerly persons subject to the defilements.[65]

b. Insatiable effort

In working for others, one should never think that one has achieved enough. Instead one should be determined to accomplish ever more virtuous behaviour.

As Shantideva says:

> If I feel that I never have enough sensual objects,
> Which are like honey smeared on a razor's edge,
> Then why should I ever feel that I have enough
> Merit, which ripens in happiness and peace?[66]

Thus it would be mistaken to neglect such opportunities for making merit as prostrations or tending to shrines.

c. Effort in application

One should constantly apply oneself to the overcoming of one's own disturbing emotions and the accomplishment of others' benefit. If one were to let this life pass in occupation with worldly trivia, it would, in the final end, be a matter for the utmost regret.

III. Its benefits

The benefits of effort are that all one's virtuous aspirations are fulfilled and finally one achieves buddhahood.

E. The perfection of meditation

I. Its remedial function

The perfection of meditation is the antidote to wavering mind.

As Shantideva says:

> Having developed effort in this way,
> I should place my mind in concentration,
> For the person whose mind is distracted
> Dwells between the fangs of the disturbing emotions.[67]

However, although the definitive remedy to the disturbing emotions is the acquisition of the insight that constitutes the perfection of wisdom, one cannot train in insight without the prior development of calm-abiding. It is this that is the concern of the fifth perfection, that of meditation.

As Shantideva says:

> Having understood that disturbing emotions are
>   completely overcome
> By insight endowed with calm-abiding,
> First of all I should strive for calm-abiding.[68]

The essence of calm-abiding is to rest the mind in one-pointedness upon a virtuous object, free from conceptual and emotional turbulence.

As Asanga says:

> The mind abides one-pointedly upon virtue.[69]

II. Its practice

Before one can apply the actual methods of producing calm abiding, one needs to establish supportive conditions for meditation. In order to do this one should 'isolate' one's body and mind from worldly involvements and the agitation caused by attachment to possessions and beings. To generate such detachment one can follow Shantideva's series of reflections on how such grasping restricts one to life in the same old samsaric cage.

If one prefers a more extensive set of reflections, one could utilise the teachings for those afflicted by impure vision as set out in *The Path and its Fruit*: i.e. the defects of cyclic existence, the preciousness of human birth and its impermanence and finally, action, cause and result. By means of either type of contemplation one will certainly develop an unfeigned sense of renunciation.

Subsequently, one should examine one's mind to ascertain whether it is still affected by any of the 'five obstacles'. To counter these one may apply the appropriate antidotes from among the 'eight remedies'. With this accomplished, one can proceed to the 'nine means of settling the mind', which sequence of instructions taught by Lord Maitreya comprises the specific set of techniques for the development of calm-abiding. As these methods are set out in detail in Ngorchen Könchok Lhündrup's *Beautiful Ornament of the Triple Vision*, it is not necessary to discuss them in detail here.

While the methods just mentioned represent the general system of developing calm-abiding, one should note that in his *Elucidating the Thought of the Sage*, Sakya Pandita has detailed an alternative method, focussed upon the development of bodhichitta. In this system, one meditates on loving-kindness and compassion as the preliminary stage and then on 'equalising oneself and others' and 'exchanging oneself and others' as the main stage of meditation. Such a method is in accord with Shantideva's teaching in his *Entering the Bodhisattva Career*.

The quintessence of this system of bodhichitta meditation is the oral instruction known as 'sending and taking', the name of which has now spread widely. Unfortunately, despite its fame, certain misconceptions about these methods are in circulation. Some, for instance, imagine that this is a system that can be taught to non-Buddhists. However, since it is exclusively a facet of training in bodhichitta, it is unsuitable for followers of the Lesser Vehicle, let alone those entirely outside of Buddhism.

Furthermore, one sometimes hears of ordinary people claiming that through their practice of sending and taking they actually heal others of their maladies. However, only the great noble bodhisattvas and fully enlightened buddhas can do this. For all ordinary practitioners the purpose of practising these methods is to maintain and extend their own generation of bodhichitta in order to achieve buddhahood. At that time they will be equipped with the limitless ability to benefit others.

There are also some who are reluctant to engage in such practices lest they be afflicted by the misery currently experienced by others. Such a fear betrays a regrettable misunderstanding of Lord Buddha's teaching. Since these practices are entirely virtuous actions how could suffering arise from them?

As Sakya Pandita explains:

Consider whether the wish to exchange oneself

With others is virtuous or sinful.
If it is virtuous, this is incompatible
With it being a source of pain.
If it were sinful, the exchange would have to be an
  action
Motivated by the three poisons.
However, as it does not arise from these three,
How could it possibly give rise to suffering?[70]

III. Its benefits

The temporal benefit of the accomplishment of the perfection of meditation is that one may obtain rebirth as a god in the desireless realms. The ultimate result is that one will achieve buddhahood.

F. The perfection of wisdom

I. Its remedial function

The perfection of wisdom is the antidote to ignorance, the root cause of cyclic existence and all its miseries. Only wisdom correctly discriminates the actual nature of phenomena and thus frees one from the two obscurations of disturbing emotions and nescience which are the obstacles to enlightenment. Its relationship to the preceding five perfections is to be both their beneficiary, in as much as they act as its necessary foundation, and their fulfilment, in as much as without wisdom they are incomplete.

As Shantideva says:

All of these practices were taught

By the Mighty One for the sake of wisdom.
Therefore those who wish to pacify suffering
Should generate this wisdom.[71]

II. Its practice

The essential method of developing the perfection of wisdom is to recognise that, in ultimate truth, all phenomena lack intrinsic nature. Thus a virtuous activity, such as giving, becomes a 'perfection' only when one does not cling to the mistaken notion that the 'three circles' of giver, recipient and act of giving actually truly exist. In fact, the three circles are merely the projection of a confused mind that seeks security in an illusory sense of solidity.

As Gyalse Thokme Zangpo says:

Since without wisdom the other five perfections
Are not enough to obtain perfect enlightenment,
Cultivating wisdom that does not conceptualise the
     three spheres
And incorporates means is the practice of a Conqueror's
     child.[72]

To gain this liberating wisdom the practitioner, who has developed one-pointedness of mind through the methods of calm-abiding meditation discussed in the fifth perfection, should train in the techniques of insight. Since the most detailed presentation of these methods of meditation on emptiness is provided by the Madhyamaka school of tenets, one should study the next chapter at this point. By alternating analytical and settling meditation on the various stages of this system one will come to an unmistaken realisation of the correct view of reality and thus will realise the perfection of wisdom itself.

III. Its benefits

The mundane benefit of the perfection of wisdom is the development of happiness and positive circumstances. The transcendental benefit is the achievement of Buddhahood.

4

Viewing Emptiness

As we have seen, those who have intelligent faith in the Buddha's teachings enter onto the path by the gateway of taking refuge in the Three Jewels of the Buddha, dharma and sangha. Subsequently, superior practitioners, their minds saturated with love and compassion for suffering beings, generate the precious bodhichitta and embark upon the Great Vehicle, which will convey them to buddhahood. Since the two provisions required for this journey are merit and wisdom, they gather the first of these necessities by the perfections of giving, moral discipline and patience and the second by the perfections of meditation and wisdom. In these twin endeavours such practitioners will rely upon the support of the perfection of effort.

In order to develop the perfection of wisdom fully one should study the profound precepts of the Madhyamaka school of tenets, the supreme among all philosophical systems. Only in this way can one clear away the accumulated debris of confused notions and thus attain certainty concerning the view of ultimate reality. Unless one does so, no matter how long one may meditate, genuine wisdom will not develop. Erroneous preconceptions will be too tenacious and consequently, even if experiences develop in meditation, one will misunderstand their nature, rendering them obstacles to liberation. It is for this very reason that all accomplished masters have stressed that one must establish certainty concerning the correct view as a necessary precursor to the profound meditation of vajrayana.

1. The transmission of Madhyamaka

A. The four schools of tenets

The Madhyamaka ('Middle Way') is one of four schools of tenets that arose in India after the passing of Lord Buddha. The first two to appear were the Vaibhashika and Sautrantika, whose adherents were followers of the shravaka and pratyekabuddha paths – the two spiritual careers forming the Lesser Vehicle. The third and fourth schools were the Chittamatra and Madhyamaka, whose adherents were followers of the bodhisattva path of the Great Vehicle. It is the Madhyamaka which is the supreme school of tenets, being derived from the Second Turning of the Wheel discourses such as *The Perfection of Wisdom*, characterised by Sakya Pandita as representing the definitive intent of Buddha's teaching.

In fact, just as the Vaibhashika is superior in its philosophical analysis to any non-Buddhist school, so each of the succeeding schools transcends its predecessors; thus

Sautrantika is superior to Vaibhashika and Chittamatra is superior to Sautrantika. Nevertheless, all these three are flawed in their delineation of the true nature of reality due to their common assertion that certain categories of phenomena, whether the 'irreducible' particles and moments of consciousness of the Vaibhashika and Sautrantika or the non-dual stream of consciousness posited by the Chittamatra, are truly existent. In contrast, Madhyamaka asserts that all phenomena without exception, physical and mental, gross and subtle, are empty of intrinsic nature and have no true existence.

B. The transmission of Madhyamaka in India

Though the root of the Madhyamaka is found in Lord Buddha's teachings, as we have noted above, the actual school of tenets began with the great master Nagarjuna, who flourished some three hundred and fifty years later, around the beginning of the Common Era. Having completely mastered the teachings of *The Perfection of Wisdom*, Nagarjuna expressed his realisation of the 'middle way' view transcending the extremes of eternalism and nihilism, existence and non-existence, in five major texts, the most important of which was *The Root Verses on Madhyamaka*. Subsequently, Nagarjuna's spiritual line was continued by his most important disciple, Aryadeva, from Sri Lanka, author of *The Four Hundred Verses*.

Between the fifth and seventh centuries C.E., two rival presentations of the common Madhyamaka system of Nagarjuna and Aryadeva developed. The first of these was the Svatantrika, ('those who argue by independent assertion') established by Bhavaviveka (c. 500 C.E.), author of *The Flame of Reasoning*. The second was the Prasangika ('those who argue by reduction'), developed by masters such as Buddhapalita (c. 500 C.E.), Chandrakirti (c. 600-650 C.E.) and Shantideva (685-763 C.E.).

C. The early transmission of Madhyamaka in Tibet

The transmission of Madhyamaka in Tibet began in the eighth century C.E. with the coming of the bodhisattva abbot, Shantarakshita, author of *The Ornament of Madhyamaka*. Since Shantarakshita was a follower of the Svatantrika Madhyamaka Yogachara system, it was this type of Madhyamaka that first spread in the Land of Snows. In the same period, another eminent Indian master, Jnanagarbha, together with the Tibetan, Chödro Lui Gyaltsen, also spread the Svatantrika system to a certain extent. However, two centuries would pass before the Nyingma master, Rongzom Chökyi Zangpo, would make the distinction between Svatantrika and Prasangika known in Tibet.

D. The later transmission of Madhyamaka in Tibet

The second introduction of Madhyamaka occurred as part of the 'later transmission' of Buddhism from India between the eleventh and thirteenth centuries. The first important centre of this later Madhyamaka was Sangphu, a monastery in central Tibet, founded by Ngok Lekpa'i Sherap of the Kadam School in 1073. It was there that his nephew, Ngok Loden Sherap (1059-1109), taught Bhavaviveka's Svatantrika works. Subsequently, at the time of the same institution's fifth abbot, the two great scholars, Chapa Chökyi Sengge and Patsap Nyima Drak spread the Svatantrika and Prasangika systems respectively. The appearance of Patsap's translation of Chandrakirti's *Entering the Madhyamaka* marks the true beginnings of Prasangika in Tibet. It soon came to eclipse the Svatantrika interpretation of Madhyamaka.

E. The transmission of Madhyamaka in Sakya

Madhyamaka studies in the Sakya tradition began during the period of the Five Venerable Masters. Although Sachen Künga Nyingpo (1092-1158) was the master of innumerable sutra and tantra teachings, his studies in Madhyamaka seem to have been confined to the Svatantrika. His principal master in this line was Tsen Khawoche. However, his son, Sönam Tsemo (1141-1182), received both Svatantrika and Prasangika teachings during his time at Sangphu, as is evident from his commentary on Shantideva's *Entering the Bodhisattva Career*. All three of the succeeding patriarchs, Jetsün Drakpa Gyaltsen (1147-1216), Sakya Pandita (1182-1251) and Chögyal Phakpa (1235-1280), demonstrated a familiarity with both Svatantrika and Prasangika in their works. Later on, in the fifteenth century, the Madhyamaka line of the Five Venerable Masters was maintained and spread widely by the peerless philosopher Gorampa Sönam Sengge (1429-1489) at a time when idiosyncratic versions of Madhyamaka were rapidly gaining ground.

It is the position of these Sakya masters that the ultimate object of the Madhyamaka view is the true nature of reality free from all elaborations, most importantly those which depict phenomena possessing either true existence, true non-existence, both true existence and true non-existence or having any other characteristic in regard to existence and non-existence.

As Chögyal Phakpa declares:

> When one recognises that all phenomena are primordially unproduced, essenceless and completely unelaborated, there is nothing to focus upon, just as with space.[73]

The true nature of phenomena, being by its very nature devoid of any characteristics by which it might be apprehended, eludes all language and all conceptual formulation. In fact, it is this conceptualisation and its ensuing manifestation in language which perpetuate the ignorance that causes us to apprehend phenomena as having true existence, which mistaken apprehension, in turn, triggers the emotional turbulence and actions that imprison us in samsara. Thus the only way to free ourselves from the cycle of birth and death is to sunder all conceptual labelling of phenomena in the unmodified direct experience of reality.

This definitive Madhyamaka upheld in Sakya is known as 'the middle way free from extremes'. As Gorampa pointed out, this is the very same Madhyamaka that was propagated by Nagarjuna and Aryadeva in India and, in Tibet, by Marpa and Milarepa and many others. It seems that, later on, even such thinkers as Jamgön Ju Mipham of the Nyingma school were influenced by this unexcelled system.

2. The teachings

A. The two truths

According to the Madhyamaka system, as with all schools of Buddhist tenets, two levels of truth, conventional and ultimate, must be distinguished. These two truths are the basis of Lord Buddha's teaching itself.

As Aryadeva says:

> The teaching of the buddhas is based on two truths:
> Worldly conventional truth and ultimate truth.
> Those who do not know the difference between these
>   two truths
> Will not realise the profound reality taught by
>   Buddha.[74]

In presenting a Madhyamaka definition of the status of conventional and ultimate truth, Sakya Pandita declares:

> 'Conventional truth' designates that which is perceived as existent in a non-analytic cognition and 'ultimate truth' refers to the non-finding of any existent phenomena in an analytic cognition.[75]

Furthermore, on this distinction between the two truths, Chandrakirti says:

> It is said that all phenomena possess a double essence:
> As seen by those who see phenomena accurately
> And as seen by those who are deluded.
> Objects of accurate perception are suchness

And those of deluded perception are conventional
  truths.[76]

According to Chandrakirti one must also distinguish
between two kinds of conventional truth – 'mistaken' and
'unmistaken':

  False seeing has two aspects:
  One with clear and one with defective faculties.
  The understanding of the person with defective
    faculties
  Is mistaken when compared to the one with clear
    faculties.[77]

Thus, 'unmistaken' conventional truth objects are those
appearances perceived by valid but non-analytical
cognition. If examined, such an object would not withstand
analysis as an intrinsically existent phenomenon, whether
because it is a mere assemblage of parts or because it
originates through dependence on causes and conditions.
However, when perceived through the valid cognition of
undamaged senses or inferential reasoning but without
such a deconstructing analysis, it would appear as existent.
  As Sakya Pandita says:

  'Unmistaken' conventional truth objects are
  appearances perceived by valid cognition, arising from
  the common consensus of beings, which are capable of
  meaningful function but which, upon analysis, cannot
  be found to be truly existent. 'Mistaken' conventional
  truth objects are appearances in non-valid cognition,

which are not capable of meaningful function, like two
moons, falling hair, mirages and so on.[78]

and Chandrakirti says:

Therefore that which worldly people perceive with six
     clear senses is true for the world.
The conceptual discussions of tirthikas created by
     delusion,
Such as the self, illusions and mirages,
These things are equally unreal for worldly people.[79]

Finally, it might be asked whether, since conventional truth
is that which is predicated on the basis of concepts and
language, ultimate truth is actually cognisable. One might
cite here Shantideva's dictum:

The ultimate is not an object of cognition.[80]

However, according to my masters, Shantideva's words
should not be understood to signify that the ultimate is
forever unknowable but, rather, that it is inaccessible to
dualistic cognition. After all, if this were not the case,
liberation from nescience would be impossible.

B. The two types of selflessness

In the discourses that belong to the First Turning of the
Wheel, the absence of a truly existent self within the five
aggregates is presented as ultimate truth. It is one's
grasping at and cherishing of this fictive self that is the
fundamental source of suffering, since when one posits a

truly existent self one necessarily also distinguishes this self from other. Such dualistic perception then acts as the ground of the disturbing emotions of attachment and aversion and so on. Consequently, these prompt the commission of erroneous actions, which in turn establish the pattern of samsaric existence.

However, in the Second and Third Turnings of the Wheel the analysis of reality that is presented is even more subtle and profound. Thus here, although various ways of understanding conventional truth are set forth, the lack of selfhood in all internal and external phenomena is taught as ultimate truth.

In accord with these two ways in which selflessness or emptiness is understood according to the Three Turnings of the Wheel, the method of realising ultimate truth taught in the Madhyamaka treatises commences with analytic meditation on personal selflessness and is then extended to an analysis of the selflessness of all phenomena.

I. Personal selflessness

The five aggregates of form, feeling, perception, formations and consciousness comprise the totality of conditioned physical and mental phenomena. As that is the case, one examines them to see if a truly existent self—an entity defined as permanent, singular and autonomous—can be located, whether identical to the aggregates or residing, in some manner, distinct from them. If it cannot be found, when one makes this comprehensive analysis of all possible modes of its alleged existence, one will have to abandon any notion that such an entity exists.

As it says in *Entering the Madhyamaka*:

> Since any self distinct from the five aggregates is not proved, it is the aggregates themselves which are the basis of the view of self.[81]

Thus when one examines the aggregates as a possible location for selfhood, one discovers that they, either singularly or collectively, cannot serve such a purpose, because each aggregate is multiple, impermanent and lacks autonomy. Yet, as has been noted above, these attributes of singularity, permanence and autonomy are precisely the characteristics that would function as the defining characteristics of any 'self'.

As it says in *Entering the Bodhisattva Career* concerning the aggregate of form:

> Teeth, hair and nails are not the self; the self is not bones and blood; it is neither mucus nor is it phlegm; nor is it lymph or pus. The self is not fat nor sweat; the lungs and liver also are not the self, neither are any of the other inner organs; nor is the self excrement or urine. Flesh and skin are not the self; warmth and wind are not the self; neither are the bodily cavities the self and at no time are the six types of consciousness the self.[82]

As it says in *Entering the Madhyamaka* with regard to all five aggregates:

If the aggregates were the self, as they are multiple, the
self would have to be multiple.[83]

However, if, in order to avoid this fault, one posited a self
distinct from the aggregates, such a self would be merely an
arbitrary designation and unrelated to actual experience,
since such experience only takes place in the aggregates. It
would therefore be utterly redundant.

As Chandrakirti says:

Apart from the aggregates there is no self, because
there is nothing established that may be perceived
independently of the aggregates.[84]

The most extensive presentation of this reasoning that
destroys belief in the notion of a self is the 'Twenty Vajra
Bombs', found in Chandrakirti's *Entering the Madhyamaka*
and Nagarjuna's *Letter to a Friend*.

In the latter text it says:

Form is not the self; the self does not possess form.
Form does not belong to the self, nor does the self
    belong to form.
In the same manner the other aggregates
Should be understood as being nothing in themselves.[85]

and in *Entering the Madhyamaka*:

Form is not the self; self does not possess the form. Self
is not in the form and the form is not in the self. Thus
under these four aspects one should know the other

aggregates. These are the twenty varieties of the view of self. These are the peaks of the mountains of the transitory collections, which are simultaneously destroyed by the knowledge of the non-existence of self.[86]

In whichever way one tries to establish the reality of a self in dependence upon aggregates, whether as identical to them or as distinct from them, one will fail. Yet, as the aggregates comprise the totality of conditioned phenomena, unless one can do this, any attempt to establish a self is doomed to failure. In short, one can only conclude there is no self distinct from the aggregates but, nevertheless, neither is there a self which is identical to them, for the reasons shown previously.

II. Phenomenal selflessness

It is, however, insufficient to recognise merely the absence of selfhood in the individual person. If one were to remain at this point, attachment and aversion to internal and external phenomena, still mistakenly understood to be truly existent, could arise. Instead, one should strive to realise that all phenomena, not just the individual self, lack intrinsic nature and, being thus essenceless, are utterly devoid of any 'selfhood' by which they might be grasped.

As Chandrakirti states:

Selflessness is [taught] for the liberation of beings. Phenomena and individual person are the two stages [of it]. Therefore the Teacher taught his disciples according to these two stages.[87]

71

In the Madhyamaka treatises composed by the great masters in India, five logical arguments, enabling one to establish the emptiness of phenomena, have been presented:

1. the 'vajra slivers';
2. refuting origination from existence or non-existence;
3. refuting origination from the four possibilities;
4. freedom from singularity or multiplicity;
5. the reasoning of dependence.

In the Svatantrika system these five methods are understood as independent assertions, while the Prasangikas define them as arguments that depend upon reasoning presupposed by philosophical adversaries, and which, therefore, function only by reducing any position maintained by such an adversary to absurdity. One can note in passing here that, whereas some thinkers in Tibet have posited a major philosophical distinction between these two systems, the majority of Sakya masters have located the difference between them as consisting, in the main, of their differing methods of argumentation as illustrated in their particular approaches to these five logical proofs.

Thus the Svatantrikas argue that a follower of a non-Madhyamaka system, who, ipso facto, does not hold the view that all phenomena are empty of intrinsic nature, can be convinced of the truth of emptiness by proofs which are reliant on independent assertion. Such a proof is exemplified in the following four-limbed syllogism, employed to prove the thesis that all phenomena lack intrinsic nature by reason of their dependence:

> All phenomena [the subject] are empty of intrinsic nature [the predicate], because they are dependent [the reason], like darkness upon light [the example].

As an example of the Prasangika method, one can follow the manner in which the 'vajra slivers' is employed by Chandrakirti in his *Entering the Madhyamaka* to render impossible any thesis maintained by an adversary. Here such philosophical adversaries are all non-Madhyamaka thinkers. As Chandrakirti demonstrates, one should enquire of such people how phenomena, which, it is claimed, possess intrinsic nature, could possibly originate, for, if their mode of origination cannot be discovered, the very notion that they exist and cease can be discounted.

In attempting to reply to this query, such proponents of intrinsically existent phenomena have only four alternatives:

a. that an intrinsically existent entity originates from itself;
b. that it originates from another distinct entity;
c. that it originates from both itself and another; and
d. that it originates without causes.

a. If someone were to assert the first of these alternatives, as do followers of the Samkhya system and others, he would incur the fault that such a mode of origination would ensure an endless reduplication of entities, thus denying the change that actually characterises the world.

As it says in *Entering the Madhyamaka*:

> If one claims that a thing already produced could be produced again, there would not be the production of a 'sprout', since the 'seed' would be never ending until the limit of samsara.[88]

Furthermore, such a theory of origination would be contradictory to reason, since it would render cause and effect identical:

> If seed and shoot are not different as you maintain, then when one does not see the seed how could one see the shoot? If they are the same, one should see them at the same time.[89]

If such were the case, the following disastrous consequence, pointed out in *Entering the Bodhisattva Career*, would necessarily ensue:

> If the effect abided in the cause, to eat food would be to eat excrement.[90]

b. Many thinkers, including theists, materialists, Vaibhashikas, Sautrantikas and Chittamatrins, assert in various ways that one intrinsically existent entity can originate from another distinct, intrinsically existent, entity. However, asserting such a position incurs the fault that, if such a type of origination occurred between unrelated entities, any entity could arise from any other entity, thus violating the continuity that exists between cause and effect.

As it says in *Entering the Madhyamaka*:

> If one entity is produced from another entity, any fruit
> could arise from any cause, like darkness arising from
> a fire's flames.[91]

Thus, whether it is theists asserting creation of the world by a creator god, materialists claiming that non-conscious matter can produce formless consciousness, Vaibhashikas and Sautrantikas alleging that, after one distinct moment of consciousness has ceased, another moment of consciousness will arise or Chittamatrins asserting a truly existent mind as the base of all, all violate this principle.

c. The third alternative offered by some opponents would be the claim that intrinsically existent entities originate both from themselves and things that are distinct from themselves. However, such a proposition incurs a double fallacy, since both of these possible modes of origination have been disproved already.

As Chandrakirti says:

> Origination from both is inadmissible because the
> faults of both have already been explained.[92]

d. The fourth and final alternative is to argue, as the Charvakas and other sceptics have done, that phenomena originate without any cause. However, such an arbitrary and chaotic mode of origination is utterly contradictory to our empirical observation of how the world works.

As it says in *Entering the Madhyamaka*:

> If the world was empty of causes, a sky flower would have perfume and colour. In fact, the world is perceived in its variety. Recognise that the world depends on causes.[93]

Thus one cannot establish the origination of an intrinsically existent entity in any manner whatsoever. One might well ask at this point, 'How then do phenomena arise?'

In reply, Chandrakirti declares:

> Phenomena arise neither without a cause nor from a cause such as God, from self, from other or from both of these, but through dependence.[94]

Out of the nexus of interacting causes and conditions, none of which exist inherently, arise phenomena, which are neither identical to nor distinct from their causes and conditions, just as the future life arises out of the interaction of sperm, ovum and linking consciousness. Thus one cannot isolate any entity, such as an unchanging self, which exists inherently. Yet, at the same time, the manifestation of dependently arising phenomena, as in this case of the process of rebirth, need not be denied. When the appropriate conditions assemble, apparent phenomena are produced in dependence upon this assemblage, just as one sees in the examples of a reflection appearing in a mirror or the moon's reflection in a pool of water.

As Chandrakirti says:

> Empty phenomena such as reflections arise in dependence upon the collection of causes and conditions. From empty reflections and so on a consciousness perceiving an image arises.[95]

Now it might be claimed that, in asserting the selflessness of all phenomena, one is actually establishing a mere nothingness as the nature of reality. If this were the case, one would have fallen into the extreme of nihilism. However, Nagarjuna and his spiritual sons repeatedly termed their system 'The Madhyamaka', precisely because it does not deviate into extremes. It seems that those who might fall into such one-sided emptiness are those who do not understand the union of ultimate and conventional truth, emptiness and dependent arising, which is the heart both of Lord Buddha's teaching and the thought of Nagarjuna.

As it says in *Letter to a Friend*:

> This dependent arising is the most profound and precious of the treasures bequeathed us by the Conqueror. Whoever sees dependent arising has the highest vision, for he knows reality as the Buddha does.[96]

Thus conventional truth, being the appearance of selfless phenomena through dependent arising, and ultimate truth, being the emptiness of intrinsic nature of all phenomena precisely because they only arise in dependence, are a unity. Although emptiness and dependent arising are different 'isolates', each being opposed to particular misconceptions, in the final analysis they share one reality.

C. The Madhyamaka free of all extremes

Although this means of abandoning the belief in intrinsically existent phenomena is amazing, it is insufficient as an understanding of the true import of Madhyamaka. Rather, the final meaning of Madhyamaka should be understood from the following statement of Gorampa Sönam Sengge:

> Since the purpose of the Madhyamaka is to abandon any kind of extremes as well as any kind of definitions, it is free from any extremes such as existence and non-existence, thing and no-thing.[97]

Thus, if having rejected belief in the reality of things, one clings to emptiness as a reality, one will be trapped by a very subtle conceptual type of nihilism in which one has conflated emptiness with the extreme of true non-existence. Instead, one must reject all clinging to concepts, even to the notion of the Madhyamaka view itself as constituting a position.

As Jetsün Drakpa Gyaltsen states:

> That which is free of extremes goes beyond the realm of speech. 'Madhyamaka' and 'Chittamatra' and so on are expressions, speech and words. They are conceptualising thoughts.[98]

The non-affirming negation emptiness, constituted by the two types of selflessness taught above, and so termed because emptiness is understood as the absence of true existence in the phenomena under examination, is not to be confused, therefore, with the definitive seeing of the true nature of reality, which is signified by the term 'free from all extremes'. Rather it is a 'conformative' or 'categorisable' ultimate in which emptiness is apprehended as a mental object known through the linguistic designation 'emptiness' and arrived at by deconstructing the notional true existence of phenomena.

This type of ultimate is thus an object fastened upon by a mind that has only partially abandoned elaborations but has not abandoned the elaboration of 'emptiness'. Indeed, even though many eminent masters have upheld this type of emptiness alone, it seems that many who follow this system run some risk of clinging to the ultimate as mere non-existence, as the omniscient Gorampa has pointed out.

It is this non-affirming emptiness, constituted by the two types of selflessness, that is the topic under consideration, when it is said in the discourse on *The Perfection of Wisdom* that 'emptiness is the mother common to all three careers': the shravaka, the pratyekabuddha and the bodhisattva. In fact, without understanding this emptiness, the achievement of the state of an arhat would be impossible for shravakas or pratyekabuddhas. Thus, incidentally, even though the Vaibhashika and Sautrantika schools of tenets assert the true existence of phenomena, their followers, who aspire to attain the level of an arhat, must contemplate emptiness to some degree.

However, if one were to argue that, in understanding this type of emptiness, arhats understand the true nature of reality, one would, in effect, be arguing that there is no difference between an arhat's realisation of reality and that of a buddha. In this case there would be little reason for the Great Vehicle to have been set forth. In actuality, it is taught in the sutras that the arhats on the shravaka and pratyekabuddha paths have only removed one of the two obscurations that veil the buddha nature, that of the disturbing emotions, but have not removed the obscuration of nescience. Thus, if one were to claim that these arhats have truly understood the nature of reality, one would be in error. They have merely understood emptiness as a non-affirming negation and concluded that the personal self and the five aggregates, upon which it is predicated, lack reality.

As Sönam Sengge states:

> The emptiness which is explained in the shravaka system is the non-affirming negation emptiness. Therefore there is a great difference [to the Great Vehicle].[99]

In contrast to the lesser paths, on the bodhisattva path one attains the uncategorisable ultimate, the non-conceptually elaborated understanding of reality, in which one realises that all assertions about reality, such as there being true existence, true non-existence, both, or some other possibility, are just conceptual labelling about that which is beyond all labelling. Through this unelaborated wisdom the obscuration of knowledge is removed, which removal cannot be accomplished on the paths of the shravakas and pratyekabuddhas. If one were to deny this unique realisation of the bodhisattva path and thereby claim that the emptiness realised by shravakas and pratyekabuddhas is the same as that realised by bodhisattvas, it would severely undermine the bodhisattva path, for, although there are other distinctions between the two paths, such as bodhichitta, the six perfections and the dedication of merit, the principal difference is the Great Vehicle understanding of the true nature of reality.

In this respect some have argued that it is only on the eighth bodhisattva level, achieved at the beginning of the third of the three aeons for which he must follow the path, that a bodhisattva attains definitive experience of the unreality of phenomena. However, to argue, as they also do, that shravakas and pratyekabuddhas realise the very same emptiness as the bodhisattva, leaves them in an untenable position, since, on the shravaka and pratyekabuddha paths, the state of an arhat can be attained within three lives of making the resolve to do so.

As Sönam Sengge declares:

> The claim that the shravaka arhat has completely removed the belief in the reality of phenomena, while the bodhisattva does not do so until he reaches the eighth level, is a denigration of the Great Vehicle.[100]

If an arhat's recognition of the emptiness of phenomena were the same as the realisation of the definitive nature of reality that arises in a bodhisattva on the eighth level, the consequence would follow that, having swiftly attained the status of an arhat, he could thus transfer directly onto the eighth bodhisattva level and, thereby, bypass the first two aeons of the bodhisattva training. To assert such a theory would therefore be, as Sönam Sengge pointed out, to damage the Great Vehicle and to render much of its training redundant.

Thus one must accept that the definitive, uncategorisable ultimate, the Madhyamaka free from all extremes, is unique to the Great Vehicle and is definitively realised only by bodhisattvas from the first level onwards. However, although its definitive realisation belongs only to bodhisattvas who have attained the levels, beginners on the path should still make it the object of their training in order to plant the seeds for its authentic realisation.

Some might argue at this point that, in describing the non-affirming emptiness as not being the definitive realisation of the ultimate, one's view becomes identical to that expressed by Dölpopa Sherap Gyaltsen and other philosophers of the 'extrinsic emptiness' system, so exaggeratedly criticised by many Tibetan masters in the name of Prasangika. In reply to this charge, one might concede that there does indeed seem to be a certain resemblance between the extrinsic emptiness system and our Madhyamaka view, particularly when, in the context of expounding the vajrayana, the latter is expressed as the union of luminosity and emptiness, which being the actual nature of mind is the 'causal lineage of the all-base', the very foundation of both samsara and nirvana.

However, despite the subtlety of the extrinsic emptiness system and the yogic accomplishments of its adherents, it is the opinion of the majority of Sakya masters that a clear distinction can be drawn. In this respect it is well known that, in taking the words of Maitreya in *The Supreme Continuity* as being of direct meaning, Dölpopa and others have asserted that the ultimate nature of emptiness, while being void of any extrinsic conditioned phenomena, possesses the four qualities of permanence, purity, bliss and identity. Yet, in so asserting, one appears to reduce the ultimate, which, by its very nature, must be unconditioned, into a conditioned entity. In doing so, one deviates from the precise Madhyamaka view of the unelaborated ultimate by positing an emptiness, which, contradictorily, has the characteristic of true existence.

Thus such a theory cannot be identified with the unelaborated ultimate of our Madhyamaka free from extremes.

As the lord of dharma, Sakya Pandita, declared:

> Existence and non-existence cannot be attributed to the true nature of phenomena.[101]

and Ngakwang Lekpa says:

> Ascribing characteristics to reality is merely giving names to that which is perceived by spontaneously aware transcendental wisdom.[102]

5

Entering Vajrayana

1. The transmission of the vajrayana

All the eighty four thousand teachings bestowed by Lord Buddha were given in accord with the mentalities of his disciples. In this respect, the first twenty one thousand of these teachings, which comprised the 'basket' of the vinaya (discipline), were primarily concerned with moral training, the antidote to the disturbing emotion of attachment. The second set of twenty one thousand teachings, which collectively made up the 'basket' of sutra (discourses), dealt mainly with meditation, the antidote to the disturbing emotion of aversion, and the third set of twenty one thousand teachings, which comprised the 'basket' of abhidharma (further dharma), was concerned with wisdom, the antidote to the disturbing emotion of ignorance. The final set of twenty one thousand teachings comprised the tantras, the scriptural source of the vajrayana; these were delivered as the antidote to all three disturbing emotions: ignorance, attachment and aversion.

At the time of teaching the tantras, Lord Buddha manifested the blissful form of a sambhogakaya buddha, endowed with the 'five certainties' of body, location, teaching, disciples and time. He first presented the vajrayana in bestowing *The Guhyasamaja Tantra* on King Indrabhuti of Öddiyana, who had requested a method of obtaining enlightenment without the necessity of abandoning sensual experience. On receiving this tantra, the monarch was liberated while remaining in the midst of his retinue of queens. Later, following Lord Buddha's passing, just as the sutras of the Lesser Vehicle were collected by the five hundred arhats and the Great Vehicle sutras were collected by the bodhisattvas, *The Guhyasamaja* and other tantras were collected by Vajrapani, the lord of secrets, and preserved in such countries as Öddiyana and Shambhala before being disseminated more widely in India by the great siddhas such as Luipa, Nagarjuna, Chilupa and Virupa.

Subsequently, between the eighth and thirteenth centuries, many tantras and their cycles of instruction were spread in Tibet by various Indian masters and their Tibetan disciples. The Sakya tradition, in particular, became the holders of a veritable ocean of such tantric teaching. However, it placed a particular emphasis upon the transmission of five major deities and their cycles: Vajrakilaya derived from the lineage of the siddha Padmasambhava; Hevajra from the lineage of Virupa; Guhyasamaja from the lineage of Nagarjuna; Vajrayogini from the lineage of Narotapa and Mahakala from the lineage of Varendraruchi. Whilst the first of these was received in the eighth century directly from Padmasambhava by Lui Wangpo, the illustrious scion of the Khön clan, and thus dates from the period of the 'early transmission' of the tantras in Tibet, the latter four were all received into the Sakya school by Lui Wangpo's kinsman, Sachen Künga Nyingpo, in the twelfth century and thus date from the 'later transmission' of the tantras. It is for this reason that Sakya, along with the Kagyu and Gelug traditions, is classed as a 'new tantra school'.

2. The relationship of vajrayana to other vehicles

Although all enter the dharma by the common door of taking refuge in the Three Jewels, two types of practitioner are distinguished amongst those who follow the Buddha: those who wish to practise the dharma primarily for their own benefit and those who wish to practise the dharma primarily for the benefit of others. As has been explained previously, in response to the first type of follower, Lord Buddha gave the teaching known as the Lesser Vehicle, a system of training by which one can win individual liberation. However, for the second type of follower, the Buddha gave the teaching of the Great Vehicle, an extensive and profound method of practice, by which one can achieve the state of buddhahood for the benefit of all beings. The motivation that animates those who choose to enter into this second vehicle is bodhichitta, an intention of total altruism causing one to strive for buddhahood in order to liberate all beings from cyclic existence.

Within the Great Vehicle itself there is a further division into two sub-vehicles: the paramitayana and vajrayana. While the motive for practice, the view of reality and the goal to be attained are common to these two systems, a major difference exists between them in respect of their modes of practice and duration of their paths.

The first of these systems is termed 'paramitayana', since the principal practices to be accomplished therein are the six perfections of giving, moral discipline, patience, effort, meditation and wisdom, which were set forth by Lord Buddha in the extensive sutras of the 'Great Vehicle'. As has been outlined above, by means of such practice, carried on throughout many lives, one is able to gather the two 'accumulations' of wisdom and merit and the causal seeds that will eventually ripen in the achievement of the two bodies of a buddha: the dharmakaya ('the truth body'), through which the welfare of oneself is accomplished, and the rupakaya ('the form body'), through which the welfare of others is accomplished. The shortest possible time in which such a result may be obtained in this system is three aeons. This gradual and incremental method of progression is the reason that the paramitayana is often designated the 'causal vehicle'.

By contrast, the second system, the vajrayana, makes it possible to achieve buddhahood in one lifetime. This is because in vajrayana, rather than trying to accumulate the causal factors that will produce enlightenment in the distant future, one practises with the understanding that the very goal of practice, the state of a buddha, is already present, in a sense, within one's stream of being. Thus, the vajrayana may be described as the 'fruition vehicle' in contrast to the paramitayana, which, as has been stated, is known as the 'causal vehicle'.

3. The special characteristics of the vajrayana

Vajrayana is so termed because, by relying on its methods, one's apparently ordinary body, speech and mind are transformed into the indestructible reality of a buddha's vajra body, speech and mind – a transformation made possible by the very fact that these nirvanic potentialities are latent within one's presently samsaric stream of being.

On this transformative characteristic of vajrayana, Lopön Sönam Tsemo says:

> At first, until one has developed bodhichitta, one trains in the same way as on the paramitayana. Then, at the time of letting him enter the mandala and bestowing initiations upon him, the vajra-master blesses the body, speech and mind of his student to become the vajras of the body, speech and mind of the buddhas.[103]

The term 'tantra', used to designate the scriptural sources of vajrayana, also illustrates the special features of this system.

As Lopön Sönam Tsemo says:

> 'Tantra' signifies the continuum of the non-dual mind, existing from beginningless time in an unbroken continuity until buddhahood.[104]

Thus, in both sentient beings ('the phase of the basis') and buddhas ('the phase of fruition') there exists the same nature of mind, the non-duality of luminosity and emptiness. As this is the case, there is no radical discontinuity between the mind of a buddha and that of an ordinary being.

As *The Hevajra Tantra* says:

> All beings are buddhas but they are temporarily obscured. When these obscurations are removed, they are buddhas.[105]

Thus the one feature that distinguishes buddhas from ordinary sentient beings is the presence or absence, respectively, of the transcendental wisdom that removes the obscurations of disturbing emotions and nescience, currently veiling our mind. This gnosis arises during 'the phase of the path', where one receives and practises the ripening and liberating skilful means of vajrayana. When one's mind meets the appropriate conditions of the path in this way, buddhahood results.

As Sönam Tsemo states:

> Like a seed presently resting in a container, if one's mind, though not presently accomplished as the reality of a buddha, meets with skilful means, buddhahood arises as the fruit.[106]

Among the many different skilful methods taught in the tantras, a particularly eminent place is occupied by mantra, for in the process of accomplishing deity-yoga, the chief spiritual practice of vajrayana, one gains the qualities of the particular deity being evoked, through the recitation of the requisite mantra. Hence, the whole system may also be known as 'the mantra vehicle'.

To explain the meaning of the term 'mantra', *The Guhyasamaja Tantra* employs the following etymology:

> Whatever mind arises from the contributing conditions
>   of the sense faculties and objects is explained as
>   'man'.
> The meaning of 'tra' is protecting.
> This protection of mind is explained as the action of
>   mantras.
> Being liberated from worldly actions, the pledges are
>   guarded.[107]

Furthermore, the vajrayana is often referred to as the 'secret mantra vehicle' due to the fact that its teachings, methods and sacred objects are not to be disclosed to those lacking the requisite initiations, vows and pledges. Nowadays, there are some who have discarded this reserve but, since it was enjoined upon practitioners in the tantras themselves, it seems that to behave in such a manner is to reject the guidance of the omniscient Buddha, thus inviting the scorn of the wise.

On the subject of those who dispense with the requirement for secrecy, Jetsün Drakpa Gyaltsen says:

> Such people only appear to be vajra-masters. Either they are ignorant and incapable of any real effort or else they want fame and have no scruples about how they

achieve it. Such attitudes do not conform to that which was taught in the words of the Buddha or the great treatises.[108]

4. The four superiorities of the vajrayana

The Indian master Tripitakamala expressed the four ways in which vajrayana is superior to the non-tantric vehicles in the following verse:

> Having the same aim but being free from confusion, it is rich in skilful means and without difficulties. It is for those of sharp faculties. The mantra vehicle is sublime.[109]

A. Unconfused in its means of recognising the view

Not only is there an identity of motivation and goal between paramitayana and vajrayana but, also, the philosophical view presented in vajrayana is identical to that maintained in the ordinary mahayana. In both systems it is accepted that the true nature of reality is free from all extremes, as the profound masters of the Madhyamaka school of tenets in both India and Tibet have explained. Indeed, if one were to assert that a view higher than this unelaborated nature of reality exists in vajrayana, it would, perforce, be a view with elaboration and thus not definitive.

As Sakya Pandita has declared:

> If there existed any view higher than the unelaborated of the paramitayana, that view would become

possessed of an elaboration. If they are unelaborated, they are without difference.[110]

However, though the view is thus one and the same in the two systems, it is much easier to recognise in vajrayana. Whereas in the paramitayana the only means for ascertaining the nature of reality is the indirect and approximate one of analysis as presented in the Madhyamaka schools of tenets, in the vajrayana, through such means as the descent of blessings at the time of the 'example' wisdom, one is able to recognise the true nature directly without conceptual meditation.

As Lopön Sönam Tsemo says:

> If, at the time of the descent of transcendental wisdom at the third initiation and so on, transcendental wisdom is born in their mental continuum, the followers of the 'secret mantra' genuinely recognise the unelaborated.[111]

B. Richness in skilful means

The vajrayana surpasses the non-tantric vehicles in the range of skilful methods it provides for the achievement of both mundane and transcendental aims. For example, in order to acquire such temporarily beneficial factors as wealth and longevity, the ordinary mahayana offers such methods as generosity and protecting life. Nonetheless, despite these being virtuous actions, they must be practised over long periods of time and with great assiduity to produce the requisite fruit in future lives.

By contrast, in vajrayana there are numerous methods for attaining these powers (siddhis) very rapidly; these include such techniques as meditation on wealth deities like Dzambhala or Ganapati or meditation upon longevity deities like White Tara, Amitayus or Vijaya. Furthermore, for the swift development of such qualities as wisdom, compassion and power, the vajrayana provides such means as meditation upon Manjushri, Avalokiteshvara and Vajrapani.

Similarly, in regard to achievement of the ultimate aim of enlightenment, the means offered in the non-tantric vehicle are the slow and gradual methods of accumulating merit and wisdom. However, in the anuttara tantra of vajrayana, one is equipped with the profound techniques of the developing and completion stages of deity-yoga, which can lead to buddhahood in this very life.

C. Without difficulties

The third factor that establishes the superiority of vajrayana over the non-tantric vehicles is that the former system can be practised without the difficulties occasioned by austerity and asceticism. While in the ordinary vehicles it is necessary to restrain one's senses forcibly in order to develop detachment from objects, which are otherwise the cause of our entanglement in samsara, in the vajrayana such restraint need not be employed. Instead, by relying upon deity-yoga, all objects of the senses are transformed into aids to enlightenment and are utilised as part of the path itself.

As Lopön Sönam Tsemo explains:

As the paramitas are the way of austerity and difficult toil, there are great hardships. The follower of the 'secret mantra' attains enlightenment by easy actions.[112]

D. Practised by those with sharp faculties

The fourth and final superiority of vajrayana is that it is to be practised by those endowed with the sharpest faculties. The immensely long duration of the paramitayana path has already been mentioned but, in the vajrayana, by contrast, such is the acuteness of its practitioners' faculties that the state of buddhahood can be achieved in this very life.

As Sakya Pandita explains:

> Just as crops gradually ripen through the proper accomplishment of tilling, so full enlightenment is won through three incalculable aeons of practice, if one sets out on the path of the paramitayana. The seeds planted through the mantra system ripen to harvest within a single day. If one knows the methods of the vajrayana, buddhahood will be won in this very lifetime.[113]

5. The four sets of tantras

Indian and Tibetan scholars have proposed various ways of categorising the tantras but most masters of the Sakya, Kagyu and Gelug traditions follow *The Vajra Panjara Tantra* where four sets of tantras are distinguished: kriya (activity) tantras, charya (conduct) tantras, yoga tantras and anuttarayoga (supreme yoga) tantras, each of which contains innumerable methods for meditating upon the deities emanated by the Buddha to bestow blessings.

As it says in *The Vajra Panjara*:

> For the inferior practitioner kriya tantras were taught;
> For those who are superior the charya tantras were taught;
> For supreme beings the yoga tantras were taught;
> And for those yet more supreme the anuttara tantras were taught.[114]

Accordingly, kriya tantras place great emphasis on techniques involving ritual activity and purity. The second set, the charya tantras, share some characteristics with the preceding set and some with the third set, the yoga tantras. This third category of tantras is oriented primarily towards meditation rather than activities. Finally, the fourth set, anuttarayoga, also stresses meditation but, in addition, possesses the supreme techniques of the developing and completion stages, which make possible the achievement of buddhahood in one lifetime.

Three lines may be distinguished within anuttarayoga: 'mother', 'father' and 'non-dual' lines. The distinguishing characteristic of mother line tantras such as Chakrasamvara is their stress on wisdom. The specific characteristic of father line tantras such as Guhyasamaja is their stress on skilful means. Finally, non-dual tantras such as Shri Hevajra and Kalachakra place equal emphasis on wisdom and skilful means.

6. The means of entering vajrayana

The only way of entering vajrayana is through the receipt of initiation from a tantric master.

As the *Mahamudratilaka Tantra* states:

> Without initiation one cannot obtain powers, just as one cannot extract butter from sand.[115]

and Sakya Pandita says:

> For one to enter the vajrayana, there is no teaching but initiation.[116]

As this is so, the consequences of attempting to practise vajrayana without first obtaining initiation are very grave.

On this point Jetsün Drakpa Gyaltsen comments:

> Even if one has faith in the vajrayana, if one is not ripened by initiation but nevertheless proceeds to practise the profound meditation, the result will be nothing more than the lower realms. Therefore one should firstly receive initiation from a fully qualified lama.[117]

By contrast, through the ripening power of the initiation, one becomes qualified to practise the yoga of the deity into which one has been initiated. Such deity-yoga constitutes the chief among the skilful means contained in vajrayana for the acquisition of either mundane or transcendental powers.

Concerning the actual nature of an initiation, Sakya Pandita says:

> Initiation is the name of the technique for becoming enlightened in this very life after the seeds of buddhahood have been planted within the aggregates, elements and sense-bases.[118]

One should note, therefore, that an initiation must be an authentic ritual derived from the tantras and not a ritual derived from the personal fantasy of some soi-disant master, because only an authentic initiation performed according to the tantras establishes the appropriate dependent connection with the bodies of a buddha. Thus, the principal form of initiation is 'empowerment' (abhisheka) performed in a mandala of a deity of any of the four sets of tantras. Following such empowerment one may receive the permission-initiation of other deities belonging to that particular tantra set and, if we have received empowerment in the mandala of an anuttara mother-line deity such as Chakrasamvara, the blessing-initiation of the goddess Vajrayogini. Subsequent to initiation one must also receive the reading-transmission and instruction relevant to the deity-yoga one wishes to accomplish.

Needless to say, it is essential that the master from whom one requests initiation possess the requisite qualifications.

Concerning this, *The Fifty Verses on the Guru* describes the general characteristics of the vajra-master who bestows initiation as follows:

> One who is stable, disciplined, possessing intelligence,

Tolerance, truthfulness, being without deceit,
Knowing the application of mantras and tantras,
    Possessing
kind affection, learned in the scriptures.[119]

The principal activities of a vajra-master are to bestow initiations, explain the tantras and give the oral instructions for practice.

As Jetsün Drakpa Gyaltsen says:

> In as much as the lama bestows upon us initiation, the explanation of the tantras and the instructions, he is called the threefold lama.[120]

The vajra-master must also possess a number of special qualifications such as having received an unbroken stream of initiation from his own masters, having maintained the vows and pledges of all three vehicles, and having obtained realisation of the deities of the four sets of tantras through retreats where he has accomplished the requisite number of mantra-recitations. In addition, he will not give initiations or accomplish other tantric rituals without the permission of his own masters.

Nowadays there is some confusion surrounding these matters. For example, one sometimes meets people who imagine they can practise vajrayana without the receipt of initiation and one also hears of people claiming to teach vajrayana who neither know anything authentic nor possess any of the requisite qualifications. One even hears reports of the unqualified 'appointing' other people to teach such fake vajrayana.

7. Vows and pledges

As we have seen earlier, in the two non-tantric vehicles there are vows that the practitioner must maintain in order to create the appropriate strength and other positive conditions for accomplishment. In the Lesser Vehicle the particular vow to be guarded is the pratimoksha vow of the monastic or lay follower. In the Great Vehicle the requisite vow is that of the bodhisattva who, having vowed to achieve buddhahood for the benefit of all beings, must avoid the various downfalls and loss of bodhichitta that will destroy such a commitment.

Similarly, in the vajrayana there are vows (samvara) and pledges (samaya) to be maintained. In total these vows are the pratimoksha, bodhisattva and vidyadhara vows, obtained at the time of initiation where, in the preliminary part of the initiation, one reaffirms one's pratimoksha and bodhisattva vows and, if it is an initiation belonging to the two higher sets of tantra, acquires the vidyadhara vow. In the lower two tantra sets, the kriya and charya, one only maintains the pratimoksha and bodhisattva vows subsequent to initiation but, if one receives an initiation in the deity-mandala of a yoga or anuttarayoga tantra, one pledges to avoid the fourteen 'root downfalls' and eight 'branch downfalls'. The fourteen major pledges which constitute the vidyadhara or, as it may be termed, the vajrayana vow, are as follows:

1. Not to despise the lama
2. Not to contradict the words of the Buddha
3. Not to be angry with one's vajra brother or sister

4. Not to abandon love for sentient beings
5. Not to abandon bodhichitta
6. Not to criticise one's own or another's school
7. Not to reveal secrets to those who are not ripened [by initiation]
8. Not to despise one's own body, which has the nature of the buddhas
9. Not to doubt the perfect purity of all phenomena
10. Not to show love to harmful beings
11. Not to grasp the limitlessness of dharmas as a limit
12. Not to turn people away from their faith
13. Not to refuse to rely on the pledge substances
14. Not to despise women, whose nature is wisdom

Although the pledges of the vidyadhara vow are specific in this way only to certain initiations, there are pledges made in every initiation: some germane to the whole set of tantras from which the initiation is derived and some relevant to that particular deity. One's acceptance of the pledges and vows is affirmed during the conclusion of every initiation, where one declares: 'As the master instructs, so I will do.' Thus, to accept the pledges and vows is a very serious commitment made to the vajra-master who bestows that initiation.

'Root' downfalls are so termed because, if committed, they destroy any possibility of obtaining realisation until one's vows are restored by retaking initiation. 'Branch' downfalls, by contrast, obstruct the acquisition of powers but do not render it totally impossible. The root and branch downfalls were explained in such tantras as *The Guhyasamaja*, and authoritative commentaries on them have been composed by Jetsün Drakpa Gyaltsen and Sakya Pandita. The most effective method of maintaining one's vows and pledges is to see one's vajra-master as inseparable from the deity whose initiation one has received, since the first and gravest of all downfalls is to harbour contempt for one's vajra-master. All other downfalls follow in the wake of this.

Nowadays there seem to be a number of erroneous ideas about vows and pledges. For instance, one meets people who believe that they have pledges (samaya) to maintain towards people from whom they have not received initiation but whom they mistakenly believe to be their vajra-master. Teachers who have given refuge or monastic ordination or bodhisattva vows are indeed worthy of respect but one does not have a tantric master-disciple relationship with them, unless they have also given one initiation. Thus one cannot have pledges to maintain towards them and, consequently, one cannot commit the first root downfall of vajrayana in respect of them (let alone to those, who though claiming to be teachers of vajrayana have no qualifications in respect of any of the vehicles).

Equally there are some people nowadays who have received initiations and yet do not understand that they have made a master-disciple relationship with that vajra-master. No matter how many masters bestow initiations upon one, one has a tantric relationship with each of them that is expressed, not only in one's acceptance of pledges at the end of each initiation, but also in the accompanying verses of the request to be accepted as a disciple by the master. This verse is recited by the recipient in the concluding section of every initiation, major or minor.

Incidentally, one should be aware that mere ignorance of the pledges does not constitute an immunity to the consequences of committing a downfall, for ignorance is described in authoritative texts as the first of the four causes that can prompt a breakage of one's pledges, the others being unconcern, lack of respect and the influence of the emotional defilements.

8. The authentic path

However, if one possesses a genuine faith in the teachings of Lord Buddha, it is appropriate to take refuge and receive and maintain the pratimoksha and bodhisattva vows. With these vows and a certainty in the Madhyamaka view as one's foundation, one may enter vajrayana through relying upon a fully qualified master who bestows initiations, transmissions and instructions. If one then maintains one's vajrayana vows and pledges flawlessly, by meditating on the deities of the lower tantras one will acquire diverse powers such as the 'four activities' of pacifying, increasing, controlling and destroying and through the yogas of anuttara tantra deities such as Hevajra, Vajrayogini or Guhyasamaja one will achieve transcendental powers.

Specifically, through the development stage one will transform mundane pride into divine confidence and with this, the aggregates, elements and sense-bases of one's ordinary experience will be realised to be the mandala of the deities. Then, through gaining mastery of the channels, winds and drops in the completion stage, one will experience the four joys, through which transcendental wisdom is beheld as a reflected image.

Finally, by blending together these two stages, which themselves express the luminosity and emptiness of mind, one will experience transcendental wisdom directly and, having traversed the five paths and the ten bodhisattva levels, will attain buddhahood. Having thus realised the dharmakaya great bliss of mind itself, through the ensuing manifestation of innumerable form kayas one will benefit beings as limitless as space until samsara is emptied.

This *Rain of Clarity* was completed by Jampa Thaye on December 20th, 2004. It was composed on the basis of the wondrous teachings that I have heard from my own kind masters. May all be auspicious!

Notes

1   Maitreya, *Theg pa chen po rgyud bla ma'i bstan bcos*, Rumtek, n.d., p. 6A.

2   bSod nams rTse mo, *Byang chub sems dpa'i spyod pa la 'jug pa'i 'grel pa*, in *Sa skya'i bka' 'bum*, vol. 5, Ngawang Topgay, New Delhi, 1992, p. 467.

3   Maitreya, op. cit., p. 4A.

4   *dKon mchog Lhun grub, sNang gsum mdzes par 'byed pa'i rgyan*, Phende Rinpoche, New Delhi, n.d., p. 12.

5   *Thogs med bZang po, rGyal sras lag len so bdun ma,* Shes bya gSar khang, Dharamsala, n.d., p. 3.

6   bSod nams rTse mo, *Byang chub sems dpa'i spyod pa la 'jug pa'i 'grel pa*, p. 467.

7   Maitreya, op. cit. p. 4A.

8   As cited in dKon mchog Lhun grub, *rGyud gsum mdzes par 'byed pa'i rgyan*, Phende Rinpoche, New Delhi, n.d., p. 35.

9   Sa skya Pandita, *sDom gsum rab tu bye ba'i bstan bcos*, in *Sa skya'i bka' 'bum*, vol. 12, p. 54.

10 Sa skya Pandita, *Thub pa'i dgongs gsal, in Sa skya'i bka' 'bum*, vol. 10, p. 468

11 As cited in bSod nams rTse mo, *Byang chub sems dpa'i spyod pa la 'jug pa'i 'grel pa*, in *Sa skya'i bka' 'bum*, p. 468.

12 Sa skya Pandita, *Thub pa'i dgongs gsal*, p. 11.

13 Maitreya, op. cit., p. 40A.

14 ibid.

15 'jam mgon Mi pham, *Gateway to Knowledge*, vol. 1., Rangjung Yeshe, Boudhanath, 1997, p. 62.

16 Maitreya, op. cit. p. 40B.

17 'jam mgon Mi pham, op. cit., p. 65.

18 Sa skya Pandita, *Legs bshad rin po che'i gter*, in Sa skya'i bka' 'bum, vol. 10, p. 226.

19 As cited in sGam po pa, *Dam chos yid bzhin nor bu thar pa rin po che'i rgyan*, Rumtek, n.d., pp. 6A-6B.

20 'jam mgon Mi pham, *Gateway to Knowledge*, vol. 2, 2000, p. 105.

21 Sa skya Pandita, *sDom gsum rab tu bye ba'i bstan bcos*, in Sa skya'i bka' 'bum, vol. 12, p.7.

22 id., p. 20.

23 Sa skya Pandita, *Thub pa'i dgongs gsal*, p. 45.

24 *dGe slong so sor thar pa'i mdo*, in bKa' 'gyur, vol. ca, Ladakhi Palace edition, pp.9- 10.

25 Grags pa rGyal mtshan, *rTsa ba'i ltung ba bcu bzhi pa'i 'grel pa gsal byed 'khrul spong*, in Sa skya'i bka' 'bum, vol. 7, p. 278.

26 'jam dbyangs mKhyen brtse dBang phyug, *dPal sdom drug pa*, in *The Collected Works of Vajrayogini Sakya Tradition*, vol. 1, Sachen International, Kathmandu, 2002, p. 96.

27 Sa skya Pandita, *sDom gsum rab tu bye ba'i bstan bcos*, in Sa skya'i bka' 'bum, vol. 12, p. 84.

28 'jam dbyangs mKhyen brtse dBang phyug, op. cit., p. 459.

29 Chandrakirti, *dBu ma la 'jug pa*, Khenpo Appey, Gangtok, 1979, p. 2.

30 Sa skya Pandita, *Thub pa'i dgongs gsal*, p. 23.

31 bSod nams rTse mo, *Byang chub sems dpa'i spyod pa la 'jug pa'i 'grel pa*, in Sa skya'i bka' 'bum, vol. 5, Ngawang Topgay, New Delhi, 1992, p. 476.

32   Sa skya Pandita, *sDom gsum rab tu bye ba'i bstan bcos*, in *Sa skya'i bka' 'bum*, vol. 12, p. 27.

33   Atisha, *Byang chub lam gyi sgron ma*, in *gDams ngag mdzod*, vol. 3, Delhi, 1979, p. 4.

34   Sa skya Pandita, *sDom gsum rab tu bye ba'i bstan bcos*, in *Sa skya'i bka' 'bum*, vol. 12, p. 29.

35   bSod nams rTse mo, *Byang chub sems dpa'i spyod pa la 'jug pa'i 'grel pa*, in *Sa skya'i bka' 'bum*, vol. 5, Ngawang Topgay, New Delhi, 1992, p. 479.

36   Shantideva, *Byang chub sems dpa' spyod pa la 'jug pa*, Rumtek, n.d., p. 3B.

37   id., p. 13A.

38   id., p.14B.

39   As cited in sGam po pa, op. cit., pp. 92B-93A.

40   id., p. 93A.

41   Shantideva, op. cit., p. 2B.

42   id., p. 3A.

43   As cited in bSod nams rTse mo, *Byang chub sems dpa'i spyod pa la 'jug pa'i 'grel pa*, in *Sa skya'i bka' 'bum*, vol. 5, Ngawang Topgay, New Delhi, 1992, p. 461.

44   Nagarjuna, *mDzad pa bcu gnyis kyi bstod pa*, in *Wa na dpal sa skya'i zhal don phyogs bsdus*, Varanasi, 2000, p. 16.

45   Atisha, op. cit., p. 5.

46   Chandrakirti, op. cit., p. 6.

47   As cited in dKon mchog Lhun grub, *sNang gsum mdzes par 'byed pa'i rgyan*, Phende Rinpoche, New Delhi, n.d., p. 175.

48   Atisha, op. cit., p. 6.

49   Chandrakirti, op. cit., p. 12.

50   Shantideva, op. cit., p. 40A.

51   id., pp. 19A-B.

52   id., p. 25B.

53   Chandrakirti, op. cit., p. 5.

54 As cited in sGam po pa, op. cit., p. 104A.

55 Chandrakirti, op. cit., p. 7.

56 Nagarjuna, *Shes pa'i springs yig*, in Jamspal, Chosphel and Santina, *Nagarjuna's Letter to King Gautamiputra*, Motilal Barnasidass, New Delhi,1978, p. 73.

57 Shantideva, op. cit., p. 27A.

58 Sa skya Pandita, *Legs bshad rin po che'i gter*, in *Sa skya'i bka' 'bum*, vol. 10, p. 231.

59 Shantideva, op. cit., p. 27B.

60 id., p. 19B.

61 id., p. 71A.

62 Thogs med bZang po, op. cit., p. 4.

63 Shantideva, op. cit., p. 38B.

64 Nagarjuna, op. cit., p. 105.

65 id., p. 109.

66 Shantideva, op. cit., p. 43B.

67 id., p. 44B.

68 id., p. 45A.

69 As cited in sGam po pa, op. cit., p. 121B.

70 Sa skya Pandita, *sDom gsum rab tu bye ba'i bstan bcos*, in *Sa skya'i bka' 'bum*, vol. 12, p. 31.

71 Shantideva, op. cit., p. 59B.

72 Thogs med bZang po, op. cit., p. 5.

73 Chos rgyal 'phags pa, *rGyal po la gdams pa*, in *Sa skya bka' 'bum*, vol. 15, pp. 293-300.

74 As cited in Sa skya Pandita, *Thub pa'i dgongs gsal*, p. 121.

75 id., p. 122.

76 Chandrakirti, op. cit., p. 17.

77 id., p. 18.

78 Sa skya Pandita, *Thub pa'i dgongs gsal*, p. 122.

79 Chandrakirti, op. cit., p. 18.

80 Shantideva, op. cit., p. 59B.

81   Chandrakirti, op. cit., p. 37.

82   Shantideva, op. cit. p. 64A.

83   Chandrakirti, op. cit., p. 37.

84   ibid.

85   Nagarjuna, op. cit., p. 87.

86   Chandrakirti, op. cit., pp. 40-41.

87   id. p. 48.

88   id. p. 14.

89   ibid.

90   Shantideva, op. cit., p. 70A.

91   Chandrakirti, op. cit., p. 15.

92   id., p. 31.

93   id., pp. 31-32.

94   id., p.35

95   id., p.20

96   Nagarjuna, op. cit., p. 108.

97   bSod nams Seng ge, *lTa ba'i shan 'byed theg mchog gnad gyi zla zer*, Sakya Students' Union, Varanasi, n.d., p. 23.

98   As cited in 'jam mgon Ngag dbang Legs pa, *'khor 'das dbyer med gyi lta ba'i snying po bsdus pa skal bzang gi bdud rtsi*, hand-written manuscript, n. d., p. 7.

99   bSod nams Seng ge, op. cit., p 80.

100 id., p. 84.

101 As cited in 'jam mgon Ngag dbang Legs pa, op. cit. p. 7.

102 op. cit., p. 6.

103 bSod nams rTse mo, *rGyud sde spyi'i rnam par gzhag pa*, in *Sa skya'i bka' 'bum*, vol. 3, p. 31.

104 id., p. 115.

105 As cited in bSod nams rTse mo, *rGyud sde spyi'i rnam par gzhag pa*, in *Sa skya'i bka' 'bum*, vol. 3, p. 116.

106 ibid.

107 As cited in id., p. 30.

108   Grags pa rGyal mtshan, *rTsa ba'i ltung ba bcu bzhi pa'i 'grel pa gsal byed 'khrul spong*, in *Sa skya'i bka' 'bum*, vol. 7, p. 306.

109   As cited in bSod nams rTse mo, *rGyud sde spyi'i rnam par gzhag pa*, in *Sa skya'i bka' 'bum*, vol. 3, p. 33.

110   Sa skya Pandita, *sDom gsum rab tu bye ba'i bstan bcos*, in *Sa skya'i bka' 'bum*, vol. 12, p. 58.

111   bSod nams rTse mo, *rGyud sde spyi'i rnam par gzhag pa*, in *Sa skya'i bka' 'bum*, vol. 3, p. 34.

112   id., p. 35.

113   Sa skya Pandita, *sDom gsum rab tu bye ba'i bstan bcos*, in *Sa skya'i bka' 'bum*, vol. 12, p. 46.

114   As cited in bSod nams rTse mo, *rGyud sde spyi'i rnam par gzhag pa*, in *Sa skya'i bka' 'bum*, vol. 3, p. 64.

115   As cited in Sa skya Pandita, *sDom gsum rab tu bye ba'i bstan bcos*, in *Sa skya'i bka' 'bum*, vol. 12, p. 38.

116   Sa skya Pandita, *sDom gsum rab tu bye ba'i bstan bcos*, in *Sa skya'i bka' 'bum*, vol. 12, p. 43.

117   Grags pa rGyal mtshan, *rTsa ba'i ltung ba bcu bzhi pa'i 'grel pa gsal byed 'khrul spong*, in *Sa skya'i bka' 'bum*, vol. 7, p. 367.

118   Sa skya Pandita, *sDom gsum rab tu bye ba'i bstan bcos*, in *Sa skya'i bka' 'bum*, vol. 12, p. 43

119   As cited in Tsar chen bLo gsal rGya mtsho, *Shes gnyen dam pa bsten par byed pa'i thabs shlo ka lnga bcu pa'i 'grel pa dngos grub rin po che'i sgo 'byed*, n. d., pp. 847-848.

120   Grags pa rGyal mtshan, *rTsa ba'i ltung ba bcu bzhi pa'i 'grel pa gsal byed 'khrul spong*, in *Sa skya'i bka' 'bum*, vol. 7, p. 251.

Made in the USA
Las Vegas, NV
07 July 2025

24523659R00066